The Administrative Challenges
of (Play) Therapy

The Administrative Challenges of (Play) Therapy

Edited by Allan M. Gonsher

Hamilton Books

Lanham • Boulder • New York • Toronto • London

Published by Hamilton Books
An imprint of The Rowman & Littlefield Publishing Group, Inc.
4501 Forbes Boulevard, Suite 200, Lanham, Maryland 20706
Hamilton Books Acquisitions Department (301) 459-3366

6 Tinworth Street, London SE11 5AL

British Library Cataloguing in Publication Information Available

Library of Congress Cataloguing in Publication Information

Names: Gonsher, Allan M., editor.
Title: The administrative challenges of (play) therapy / edited by Allan M. Gonsher.
Description: Lanham : Hamilton Books, an imprint of Rowman Littlefield, [2019] | Includes bibliographical references and index. | Summary: "This book brings together essays by eight professional child and family therapists who discuss their careers and the type of therapy they practice. The contributors focus on play therapy, the different modalities in which it is practiced, on their journeys as passionate practitioners with the goal of improving the lives of children and families"-- Provided by publisher.
Identifiers: LCCN 2019045280 (print) | LCCN 2019045281 (ebook) | ISBN 9780761871682 (cloth) | ISBN 9780761871699 (epub)
Subjects: LCSH: Play therapy. | Management.
Classification: LCC RJ505.P6 A36 2019 (print) | LCC RJ505.P6 (ebook)
DDC 616.89/1653--dc23
LC record available at https://lccn.loc.gov/2019045280
LC ebook record available at https://lccn.loc.gov/2019045281

Dedicated to all the children that inspire us with their strength.
Thank you for teaching me even more of the
power and presence of the Divine.

Contents

Acknowledgments

I would like to thank many people who have helped bring this book to fruition. Our publisher Brooke Bures, Hamilton Books, who always provided great encouragement, and Sam Brawand, who is an incredible, kind yet exacting copyeditor.

My gratitude to all of the contributing authors, who have been my friends and colleagues throughout my career, and to their families who continue to support them throughout their therapy lives' work, which is always demanding.

A special thanks to my son, Dr. Joshua Gonsher, who continued to encourage and edit the book, and to Dr. Paul Fine and Ms. Sally Fine who have been my friends, mentors and inspiration for my entire career.

And my admiration and appreciate to my wife, Rini, who has always inspired and challenged me to be my best, and of course, none of this is possible without the help of the Almighty . . . He has always believed in me and helped me throughout my personal and professional journeys.

Introduction

Allan M. Gonsher

I have been in practice as a Registered Play Therapist Supervisor (RPT/S), a Licensed Clinical Social Worker (LCSW), and a Licensed Independent Mental Health Practitioner (LIMHP) for forty years. The primary focus of my work has been to help thousands of children and families to become healthy and grow in their own lives and relationships. Along this journey, I have successfully operated two large private practices in Nebraska and Kansas, known as Kids Incorporated, that allowed me to provide professional supervision and guidance to hundreds of other clinicians, colleagues, and students in the field of play therapy. My passion as a therapist has given me the opportunity to touch and change many lives, and for this I am extremely fortunate and grateful.

As a practitioner and as a teacher, my experience can be useful for others who choose to follow a similar path in their careers. Over the years, the profession has expanded from mainly private practice to home-based services, school programs, non-profit environments, and community education. With each new opportunity, the clinical and administrative challenges have also changed to include new and different responsibilities, costs, facilities, operations, communications, and relationships. All of these are just as critical to the effective service to clients as they are to the proper conduct of business. The writings and teachings in this book will help others who have chosen a similar direction in life.

This book lays out for one who is considering or entering our profession many outstanding ideas for success. We have learned from our experiences and share with the reader how the creation of a proper therapeutic environment and persona are critical to the recovery of a client's mental health. Traveling to a safe and convenient location, having an accessible building for visitors, entering a professional office space, being comfortable in the physical arrangement of a work area, and enjoying the accoutrements of an office design all contribute to a client's positive mindset.

In addition, newcomers to the field must pay attention to the proper conduct of a business. A successful practice requires a secure financial base, sufficient insurance protection, capable and sensitive support staff, collaborative colleague relationships, efficient administrative and health care provider procedures, and a fair billing plan. It is one thing to help clients and their families confront debilitating health issues and to overcome personal challenges, but attention must also be given to the environment that nurtures this recovery so those who spend time with therapists and practitioners can do so in a safe, comfortable, and atmosphere. Our experts talk about these attributes of a successful practice.

The clinicians who have contributed to this book are seasoned therapists, each with nearly two decades of experience. They have practices in various locations in the United States, in both large and small communities, and have served clients whose economic, cultural, religious, health, educational, and ethnic backgrounds are as diverse as the entire country. Some have had small, private practices, some are associated with larger groups of professionals, some are employed by public and private educational organizations, and others provide home-based services to those in need. All have received advanced degrees in several different fields of study that relate to our discipline. Most important to all of these experts in the field is that they love what they do.

In chapter 1, "From the Beginning: Private Practice," Yeshim Oz, who has practiced for more than two decades, provides her insight. Also an LIMHP, Oz, who specialized in Autistic Spectrum Disorders in her native Istanbul, Turkey, now has a practice in United States. She has had successful practices based on networking, referrals, and caseload maintenance in school, group, and private environments. In addition, she has developed an expertise in client finance and insurance issues that strengthen both the service and the business aspect of her practices.

Julie Plunkett's chapter 2, "Private Practice, Agency, Adjunct Professor: Diversity in Therapy," discusses the transitions that occur in different positions of practice as one progresses in a career. She represents the professional person whose interests, motivations, and personal circumstances change over time. Plunkett has been a Licensed Professional Counselor (LPC) in various disciplines and speaks to her own professional and personal experiences as she became a program administrator and professor teaching others about the journey.

With over two decades of play therapy experience, Amy Hyken-Lande has specialized in divorce, trauma, PTSD, domestic violence, coping skills, and social and self-esteem issues for her patients' health and well-being. She has worked in all clinical environments to navigate sensitive interpersonal relationships among her colleagues to manage their challenges, obstacles, production, and enjoyment of the profession. In chapter 3, "Variations of a Theme: Private Practice," Hyken-Lande shares her experiences moving from graduate school to earning her LCSW to her path to private practice.

Amy Badding exemplifies the world of a respected Licensed Mental Health Counselor (LMHC) and an RPT by incorporating life balance to her profession, clients, and family. In chapter 4, "Navigating the Challenges of Being a Parent and a Play Therapist," Badding provides some insight into the combined roles of therapist and that of parent. With strong clinical credentials and experience, she capably separates her association with the University of Nebraska Medical Center and practice as Parent-Child Interaction Theraphy (PCIT) trainer from her active role as a mother. Badding teaches us about the need to protect personal privacy and maintain self care in order to perform professional duties properly.

In chapter 5, "In-Home Therapy," Jacquelyn Thompson describes a new generation of service delivery for a new generation of clients. Thompson has been practicing for more than a decade and holds licenses in Nebraska as a Licensed Independent Mental Health Provider (LIMHP), Licensed Mental Health Practitioner (LMHP), Certified Mater Social Worker (CMSW), and Licensed Alcohol and Drug Counselor (LADC). She provides insight into the operational, therapeutic, and economic differences between those who visit a private practice or agency and those who choose to remain in a homelike safe haven to visit with their therapist. She also discusses issues of cleanliness, safety, and privacy as topics of importance for both the therapist and the client.

Amanda Gurock (LICSW), writes in chapter 6, "From Private Practice to an Agency to a Clinic: Trials and Tribulations," about the distinction between moving from private practice to creating an agency, which is now accepted as a clinic. With over fifteen years of experience with her own private practice, she brings to the discussion her training as a Trauma-Focused Cognitive Behavioral Therapist (TF-CBT) and a Child-Centered Parent Teacher. Her understanding of financial responsibilities and multi-office physical plants will help one develop a successful business.

In chapter 7, "School-Based Therapy," Dianna Sawyers (LIMHP, LCSW) introduces the education environment as the focus for providing Play Therapy for young clients. As a school counselor, her insights into communication with school officials and relationships with teachers and administrators who may not understand the concept of Play Therapy will be revealing to support a workplace atmosphere that is very different than the traditional private practice office. Sawyers shares with the reader the additional challenges of play rooms inside classrooms, vacation and holiday interruptions, and caseloads to meet academic and student schedules.

My chapter 8, "Private Practice and Consulting," provides insight on the journey as a practitioner specializing in Play Therapy, to the formation of a private practice and consulting firm, and a discussion of the practical financial considerations. The chapter provides useful advice for those who wish to serve their patients, impart their knowledge to others by speaking and consulting, and provide for their families in meaningful ways.

I want to express a special thanks to the Association of Play Therapy (APT; www.a4pt.org) for always demanding excellence in what we as licensed practitioners do for others and for ourselves. My appreciation is also extended for the encouragement and camaraderie of my faculty and staff and all the associates with whom I have shared my gratifying career. And my true inspiration for my ability to love and embrace life has been from my wife Rini, my children, and my grandchildren. Of course, none of this is possible without the help of the Almighty.

My mantra has always been, "If we save one child's life, we have saved the entire world." That thought has been with me every day during my career. It has driven my actions, my decisions, my relationships, and my goals on this earth. I share it with you so you may do the same.

ONE

From the Beginning

Private Practice

Yeshim Oz

When I was asked to share my ideas for a book about the administrative aspects of private practice, I started to reflect on which of my experiences that might be useful for young professionals contemplating the same path. Several years ago, my only compass was what I learned from colleagues and mentors, mostly in the form of good conversations over coffee or lunch. There was no book that could answer my questions or ease my anxiety. In this chapter, I intend to share my experiences with the hope of providing the reader with practical information.

We clinicians generally spend a great deal of time, energy, and money to become better at what we do through books, study groups, workshops, and certification trainings. Being a good therapist is what we focus on and, unfortunately, we often exclude all other aspects of our professional world such as running a business. Yes, having a private practice is essentially running a business that requires a well-managed budget, a well-maintained office, web presence, and a good billing and collection system.

BACKGROUND

I started my counseling career as an elementary-school counselor. Knowing that I was more interested in psychotherapy, I accepted a part-time therapist position in a group practice that was a great referral source and offered regular clinical and administrative supervision meetings. I could not have asked for more. I became credentialed and was able to accept clients with insurance. Having a full-time position in a school system made the transition to another sphere within the profession easier, especially in terms of finances. While I was getting experience and a flavor of what it meant to be a therapist, I did not have to worry about money. When I had a large enough case load, which was around eighteen to twenty-two sessions per week, I resigned my position at the school to become a full-time therapist. In the new location, I was working in a group practice as an independent contractor. I learned from more experienced therapists in the group. It had been an incredibly rich experience which prepared me to dare to spread my wings and open my own private practice. I deliberately used the word *dare* because the anxiety caused by the unknown, as well as the desire to be one of those *cool* psychotherapists we see in some television shows who successfully help their patients, guided me through this painful, but hopeful process. Any beginning, any endeavor for something new, can be scary. Certainly, the encouragement generously given to me by my colleagues was absolutely essential for me to feel that I could be successful.

FINANCES

One of the first lines of business is to do the math: How much am I making with a moderate case load (that is, eighteen to twenty-two weekly sessions)? What is the average overhead cost for private practice (for example, rent, utilities, advertisement, website, billing, workshops)? Can I live comfortably after saving for retirement and paying for health insurance? To do the math, I had to have a good idea of the average insurance reimbursement per session and the average number of sessions per week that were possible. Once I figured out my possible weekly base income, the rest was to multiply this number with the number of weeks in a year that I was willing to see clients. To be on the safe side, I took ninety percent of it. The result of the math was positive for me. I could potentially earn as much as I was making at school, so I started to look for an office space. There might be geographical differences, but in my Midwest city, most therapists huddled together in certain buildings and areas. I rented an office in one of those buildings because for me (1) private practice can be lonely, so having colleagues around even to chit chat while warming up lunch in the kitchen is helpful to reset the mind for the next client; (2) networking with colleagues becomes much more important when working solo; and (3) having colleagues with different specialties in the building would make the referral process easier and, as a result, the community is served better.

TRANSITIONING

When transitioning from one setting to another, which, in my case, was from group to private and solo practice, one has to be financially ready. Although I already had a fully decorated office within the group practice, I needed to purchase new furniture for a waiting room. If you get to be as lucky as I was and the leasing market is not very competitive, you will only need the first month's rent and a security deposit. I can imagine the market situation can be quite competitive in bigger cities, so to eliminate at least one stressor during the transition phase, it is advisable to have a few thousand dollars extra because the first reimbursements from insurance companies can be delayed for many reasons, such as address or tax ID number (state and/or federal) changes. It is naive to think that the transition will be smooth and without any glitches. What I particularly want to emphasize here is the bureaucratic procedures. This can involve providing insurance companies your new tax ID number and completing all the necessary forms to be recognized as a new entity at least a few months ahead of time so you will get reimbursed without any delay. I spent my first few months quite worried in terms of income. However, as the referrals from colleagues and the Internet continued, mostly for reasons I explain below, within a year I was quite established with a moderate case load.

REFERRALS

That brings me to the topic of referrals. This is the most important aspect of the private practice business. Ultimately, your income depends on clients finding you, one way or another.[1] The question is: how can you make your community aware of your services? A strong Internet presence is a must in this era of technology. People use Google and other search engines. Being on one or more therapist directories is a good starting point. There are a few widely used directories that worked well for me but research for yourself which are the best for your field and area. For a small monthly fee, I had already been listed in a directory. In addition, a website that is connected to your profiles in these directories can be very helpful, especially in explaining your services and your expertise in details. Upon the recommendation of a colleague, I enrolled in a web-based billing system through which I could make the appointments, upload my new-client forms, submit claims, and keep records of all money affairs. As a solo practitioner, using a web-based billing system seemed to be my best option because I did not have a budget to hire a healthcare billing specialist. Also, the services I received for a minimal monthly payment served all my needs. It took a few weeks to learn how to navigate the website, but afterwards, submitting claims is just one click away.

I really found it easy and useful. I also had my website prepared by the same company for a very low monthly payment. Later, I also added a blog page to my website to increase the traffic. In the beginning, the Internet was the major referral source. Currently, after several years in business, I have become better known by the therapy community. At present, my colleagues are my main source of referral. For that to happen, I felt it was necessary for me to be active and participate in study groups, professional associations, online forums, and discussion groups.

When choosing a discussion or study group, I believe it is just natural to go in the direction you want to grow as a professional. Psychoanalysis and psychodynamic psychotherapies, including Jungian analytic psychology, have always been my passion. I also continue to have coffee and lunch with groups of colleagues, in order to exchange ideas and information, and to keep up with the current happenings in the psychotherapy community. I realized that former clients can be quite important in getting new clients as well. In other words, I suggest not overlooking the importance of a good job done a few years back. From time to time, I receive a telephone call giving me the name of a former client as a referral. That feels really good!

One caution about referrals: I cannot yet figure out any reason for this pattern, but there are periods of silence (that is, the telephone has not been ringing for a few months) followed by a flux of calls. When I first experienced the silence, I panicked. What helped me calm down were the words of a beloved supervisor telling me exactly what I had just said. It was a relief knowing that the periods of not getting any calls happen even to the seasoned, well-known therapists. Therefore, expect this kind of cycle and do not panic!

Last but not least, in terms of referral source, you should have a niche or expertise in one particular area. In my case, it is psychoanalysis. When I started my training at the Greater Kansas City Psychoanalytic Institute, I was one of the few therapists in my town who could offer psychoanalysis. In fact, I was the only one in the directory of the American Psychoanalytic Association (APsaA). As a result, I attracted clients who were especially interested in a more intense, long-term form of treatment. My passion in psychoanalysis led me to meet like-minded professionals in that community. This eventually helped me realize the importance of pairing with a psychiatrist. Psychiatrists can be a steady and solid referral source if they are convinced that you can help their patients. One caution about this point though is to find someone who values psychotherapy. Unfortunately, the number of psychiatrists who rely on managing mental illnesses solely with medication is quite high. Your task should be to find one who does value psychotherapy and who believes that the *prescription* for a real and long-lasting healing should also include a psychotherapeutic process.

CASELOAD

When it comes to caseloads—in other words, how many weekly sessions you should conduct—it depends entirely on your capacity to do the work without compromising. For some, it could be more than thirty-five; for others, it may be only fifteen to twenty. My magic number, which I happened to discover having worked several years in the field, is six sessions per day. I see patients Monday through Thursday, and Friday is assigned for study groups or rescheduling if necessary. I prefer to have three sessions in the morning and three in the afternoon after a one-hour break for lunch. This is how I feel my best, and I want to offer my best to all my patients, whether their session is the first or the last in the flow of the day. This by no means is to say that it is true for everyone. I know many successful therapists see more clients a day. You will discover which schedule is best for you.

One thing to remember about the caseload is to expect fluctuation. Of course, we try to minimize the possibility of having fewer sessions per week than desired. I accept new patients and work more hours than ideal if I know that termination of counseling process is near for some existing patients. However, I still have down time, especially around the holidays and summer months. In time, I discovered that this is actually a blessing in disguise because when I first started my private practice, I saw patients even on the 4th of July, not giving myself a much-needed and deserved break. After noticing the pattern for down time, I take my vacation around that without feeling guilty.

SUPERVISION

I am an independent practitioner; however, I always have one or two supervisors by choice. I can not emphasize enough the necessity and benefits of being in supervision with a seasoned therapist, especially for inexperienced, new clinicians. In our line of work, there is no immediate feedback on how we are doing. Supervision gives us the opportunity to review our work with an experienced clinician, who can see what we may not or cannot. This ensures that we do not overlook something serious or detrimental to our clients' situation. Beside the ethical aspect, we also learn where we stand in terms of our professional development. Private practice can be very lonely and anxiety-ridden at the beginning. One of the most important functions of a supervisor is to contain the anxiety of the supervisee and help them thread through thick woods. It is not uncommon for new therapists to just give up within the first year or so if they do not receive professional support.

PLAY ROOM

Transitioning to private practice brought a series of changes in my professional preferences. I used to see more children and families because the group practice I had worked with was known for its excellent services for children and families. My work with parents evoked a curiosity and desire to see adult clients as well. As a result, I currently see more adults than children. With that being said, I would never relinquish the play corner in my consulting room. This corner consists of a custom-made sand-play table, shelves of mini figurines, and board games. I also keep materials for creative play, such as modeling clay and drawing supplies. Since I am a psychoanalytically oriented psychotherapist, through the choice of toys or materials available, I make sure to cultivate a child-centered, non-directive approach with children, especially with those who display internalizing behaviors.

At the dawn of my practice, upon realizing my ambition to buy all kinds of toys, one of my child-therapist colleagues made a passing comment that "less is more." It turned out that this comment, far from being a passing moment, resonated with me. I later concluded that what really mattered was playfulness. The essence of play is in the imaginative process. Children reveal valuable information about their inner struggles by playing, especially when they pretend to be at school. Using my clipboard, computer paper, and pens and pencils, all simple *toys*, I accomplished what I needed. Thus, quality rather than quantity matters when it comes to what toys to include in the playroom area. I always liked the projective nature and the attraction of sand play for school-age children. Therefore, I designed the play corner accordingly.

INTAKE

Besides being technically and physically ready to see clients in your own, solo practice, another key area to successfully set the stage for a strong practice is how you handle an intake with a client. Intake starts with the first contact, whether it is an email or a telephone call. My response time is usually within twenty-four hours. I always start by thanking them for contacting me and politely asking if they have a few minutes to discuss their concerns. If it is via email, before I offer a time slot, I limit my questions to a few ones on logistics, such as what kind of insurance they have, what is their availability, and why they are looking for a therapist. My goal is to get a feel of what they are looking for and to see if I can provide it. Since I believe that every interaction has a meaning, if there is a struggle on the part of a client to find a time for the first appointment, the motivation could be weak or ambivalent. Similarly, if they do not respond to your voicemail in a timely manner (which I believe is within twenty-four to forty-eight hours), there might be some resistance.

Unlike some other settings such as agencies or clinics that might have a separate intake protocol, in private practice, the intake is the beginning of the psychotherapeutic relationship. Therefore, I pay close attention to my level of comfort with the person because this might also be diagnostically important with regard to the work. On the day of the client's appointment, I simply begin by asking them to complete some paperwork and then ask if they have any questions. Since the intake is a biopsychosocial evaluation, I inform them that in regular sessions, I do not take notes. Most clients understand this procedure. I do have a specific form for my own use that consists of a series of questions. However, I do not follow the order of the questions. I open the intake with the simple question of "What is going on?" or "What brought you here today?" With this question, I invite them to share the issues and struggles they are experiencing. I do not interrupt them. I maintain eye contact as best as I can, give them brief and encouraging nods, and use some active-listening techniques. When the client is comfortable telling me their story, the conversation flows quite naturally, and I follow their leads. Not every client is like that, so sometimes a more directive approach is indicated, especially when the client's anxiety is high and/or if I notice a strong inhibition.

With ten to fifteen minutes left before the end of the intake, I ask them how they feel about working with me and if they have questions for or about me or my approach. If their answers are on the positive side, then I suggest we meet one or two more times before laying out a treatment plan, which, besides the goals, includes the type of therapy modality (supportive psychotherapy or psychoanalysis), regular appointment times, length and frequency of sessions, payment, insurance, cancellation policy, and the diagnosis to be submitted if a third-party payment is involved. A strong position of mine is also to invite any concerns of the client that are not yet addressed before diving into the psychotherapy work. My favorite question to wrap up the evaluation is, "Can you think of anything else I haven't asked?"

On very rare occasions, however, I may have a strong feeling that we are not a match. In this case, I give the person the names and contact information of at least two colleagues. This is usually the case if I do not have enough time slots open. When the person needs a more intensive form of treatment or I think they should be treated in a clinic or hospital setting where more staff are available, I will then refer out. With all that said, one should keep in mind that this is my way of conducting the intake interview, and it developed over time and with experience. Give yourself time to create your own style.

CONCLUSION

The purpose of this chapter has been to give readers practical information with regard to forming and establishing a private practice in the field of psychotherapy and is based on my own experience. I tried to cover as many areas as possible, and you might face some unforeseen challenges due to different circumstances such as living in a different city or town that has different community needs or a different state where the operation of insurances varies. Nevertheless, one key point to take away should be that you can succeed in the establishment of a good private practice if you have good support and a passion as well as patience for it. It takes some time to develop your style. In the meantime, you should surround yourself with successful and experienced colleagues and mentors to internalize the best practices no matter what your or their theoretical orientation is.

NOTE

1. See specialized software for therapists and practices, such as *Therasoft* (www.therasoft.com); *SimplePractice* (www.simplepractice.com); *Therapysites* (www.theraphysites.com).

TWO

Private Practice, Agency, Adjunct Professor

Diversity in Therapy

Julie Plunkett

The practice of therapy has a great deal of diversity. There are many ways to practice therapy as well as a multitude of interesting clients to work with. When looking to find your place in the world of therapy, it helps to know what the different settings you might work in look like. Therapy is also an occupation that one does not leave at the office. You define your practice of therapy by who you are, and it helps us define who we will become. Trial and error are part of this journey. If I had known more from the beginning of my career, I probably would have made different choices and managed challenges differently. This chapter will teach things about working in an agency and in a university setting. The hope is that this can direct you in your future choices both professionally and personally.

BACKGROUND

My dedication to helping children and families led me to train to become a counselor. My first three years I worked with adolescents in a residential facility, and then I did contract work with a company that provided in-home therapy to children involved in the foster-care system. In these situations, I worked with children as young as three years old, but I often did not know how to help them. At this point I realized that there was more to therapy than what I learned in graduate school.

One session in particular stands out. I was in the middle of an in-home session with a five-year-old foster-care child. This particular child continued to struggle with emotional and behavioral regulation, although I felt I was making some progress; however, intuitively I knew I was not doing enough since there was so much more I could do. Early in my career, I had heard about play therapy and certification programs, but I had been too busy with the "business" of therapy and life to give it much thought. I knew at that moment that play therapy could provide many answers to my questions; the realization of the connections between my personal and professional lives, through play, influenced my future career decisions.

DUAL ROLES

In counseling dual roles are often present. One of these examples is when one could have a professional therapeutic role as well as a casual small-town interactive one. One of the most common challenges I faced professionally was when a friend wanted me to work with them and their family. Because of their trust in me and the sensitive nature of the relationship, I found this dual relationship sometimes difficult to navigate. Because I felt the personal and professional roles overlapped, I would tactfully refer them to another clinician.

Dual roles often went beyond the relationship with a client. It also included different professional and individual roles. My first dual role, professionally and personally, was when I was a student and counselor. As a lifelong student, I was learning filial therapy.[1] Filial Therapy is a type of treatment where the parents are taught the basic principles of Child-Centered Play Therapy. They are taught to structure the play time, use empathic listening skills, effectively utilize imaginary play, and to set appropriate limits. This is first modeled for them by the therapist. They then practice it under supervision of the therapist. Finally they are able to practice it in the home one-on-one with their child. The ultimate goal being to help them use this in the home managing difficult behaviors and increasing bonding.

During my class on filial therapy, a professor asked me, "What is it like to do filial therapy as a mom?" My answer was that I did not know how to answer that, but I said, "I am a mom and I am a therapist. They are not separate entities; they are both who I am." This was the first realization that balancing the roles of a clinician and a mother was something I needed to do. This was a challenging and real concept when I was in my play therapy training.

The evolution of this life challenge was intense while I was learning to do filial therapy with parents. I was also practicing it on my children, who were both in elementary school. This was the beginning of many years of growth for all of us. They both loved to have special play time with Mom but not when therapeutic skills were employed. My youngest craved the connections with me; my oldest craved the control it gave.

I will never forget the day my oldest said, "I don't want a therapy mom; I just want a mom." I recognized I needed to play different roles and learn to integrate them. Recognizing how to separate and integrate them has helped me become who I am.

My now fifteen -year-old is proud of the ability to understand therapy, discuss it with me, and help his friends. It is something that stands out from peers. What had once been contentious is now a source of bonding. I navigate that dual role fairly successfully.

One day my oldest sent me a text stating "IRL" (*in real life*, for those of you who might be as confused as I was). I admitted my ignorance and asked what it meant. My youngest piped up and said, "Mom does not understand what any of that stuff means." Qualifying it by saying, "It took me a long time to learn it too Mom. Some people just know these things, and others have to work hard at it, like Mom." I responded, "I am not, nor will I ever be, the cool mom that understands all of this popular culture stuff." My oldest immediately responded, "You *are* the cool mom! I can talk psychology with you!" The conversation continued on the topic of how cool is not the same for everyone.

This was another changing moment in my career. At a time when popular culture says that children turn away from their parents and rely more on their friends, I found it not to be true. My children do turn to me and are deepening their relationship with me. As I processed this interaction, I realized that the dual role of therapy mom and therapist that I balanced when my children were young was proving profitable; we were connecting on a meaningful level. I realized that the compartmentalization of me was not productive. Integration of me as a mom and me as a professional cannot be separate. This is a global phenomenon, and some navigate it more successfully than others. The idea of wearing different hats is a natural part of being human. In some professions it may be easier to separate one's professional or work self from one's private or home self. In the field of therapy, though, this is a larger challenge. Therapists go into therapy wanting to make a difference based on who they are as a person. Because of this, a person might struggle with the overlapping roles.

My journey continued when I evaluated my private practice that I had spent years building. Once again, the discussion on dual relationships needed to be explored.

TRANSITION

My private practice was successful. I had a good name in the community and plenty of referrals, but I was alone. As I supervised other clinicians, I realized I wanted to be in a team environment. Connection with others solidified my vision of wanting to be part of something larger, and I could bring healing to children, adolescents, and families, which could only be actualized with the support of other therapists.

Service to others has always been my focus for doing therapy. Because of this the best fit for me was a non-profit agency. For me, the benefit of working in a non-profit agency was the ability to serve families that would not be able to afford therapy in a private practice setting. This type of work was extremely gratifying and gave me additional perspectives.

TEACHING

In spite of my successes in therapy, I felt a need to teach. To those ends, I began a journey that included teaching undergraduate and graduate students and teaching webinars specifically on play therapy. A wonderful part of teaching was a chance to learn as much as the students. The challenge of balancing roles was a continuous adventure for me.

One of the classes I taught at the undergraduate level was Human Growth and Development. Through that class I was reminded once again of Erik Erikson and his Stages of Development.[2] As I taught, the opportunity to learn as a student again resurfaced, and I realized I was in the Generativity vs. Stagnation stage. At this stage a person experiences patterns of life, and society becomes a greater concern. A major task of this stage is to give back, which allows us to experience generativity; however, if we become unresponsive or unproductive, we are in stagnation.

With further introspection, I realized I was experiencing generativity. I was being productive, doing important work, gaining knowledge, and contributing to the next generation.

My life had been a series of balancing many roles and challenge. I started as a therapist-mom, I then became a therapist-supervisor, and now, I am a therapist-professor. It was a profound realization of the parallel to parents balancing their multiple roles. This balancing has made me a stronger therapist-mom, and this skill is vital to any therapist working with children, adolescents, and families.

EXPENSES/LOCATION

A benefit of both teaching at a university and working in an agency is that overhead is minimal. Both cover expenses such as rent, phones, Internet, and copying services. Physical space is usually not an issue in universities, as classroom facilities will be provided. With online classes the university will have their own protocol, whether it is on or off campus, and conducting classes from home requires you to have a computer and Internet connection. Most professors who are adjunct do not have their own office but a place where they can meet with students outside of class or do prep work as needed. Each university will have their own web-based network where assignments, grading, and communication take place. This is also available remotely.

An adjunct professor will have a limited number of classes, and scheduling will not be consistent. An adjunct faculty does not receive enough remuneration to be considered a full-time position, so, to accomplish that, one needs to work at several institutions. Again, the act of balancing plays into this role. An adjunct teaching position can add experience, diversity, and income to a full time job.

Depending on the university and the type of classes you are teaching, your liability insurance could be an issue if you are in a master's program and are teaching the practicum or internship classes. There is a difference between teaching at the undergraduate level and the graduate level. When you are an adjunct professor in a graduate program for counseling or social work liability insurance is no different than would be as a therapist though it is in addition to your insurance as a therapist. However, some universities provide liability insurance that covers an individual through their contract, but purchasing your own insurance as a supplement is worth exploring.

The issue of obtaining liability insurance needs to be addressed. Liability insurance can be a large financial investment. Some are based on how many clients you see in a week as well as the type of practice you do. When working with an agency, a benefit is that they provide it for you. Be aware though that an agency might not cover you if charges are filed against you, so you can still might want to purchase supplemental coverage. Remember, the agency will defend its needs first, not necessarily those of the clinicians. This is a discussion one should have with the agency and some of its employees before accepting a position in that agency. There are policies that cover a person but might cost less if one is part of an agency.

Liability insurance will vary based on what state you are practicing and the type of degree you have. Students also pay less for their insurance coverage. It will also depend on what amount of coverage you have. A common choice is $1 million per claim and $3 million per year as opposed to $1 million per claim and $5 million per year. If you are self-employed current rates for full time work are around $300–$350 per year. If you work for an agency that covers your insurance and you decide to supplement that with your own policy, even at full time it is going to be around $130–$150.

One last consideration when exploring university work is degree requirements. For example, I was able to teach in psychology and counseling programs because of the course work I had completed for my masters, but in another program, such as social work, I was not considered
qualified. If one is interested in teaching in some graduate programs and
especially securing full time positions, completing a PhD is essential.

AGENCY VS. UNIVERSITY

Having your own office has an advantage in how you set up the room
and availability of supplies. On the other hand, one room might not be
big enough. For example, family therapy could have different needs than
individual child therapy. By the time you arrange your toys and supplies,
it might be difficult to have a family session. When interviewing for a
position, ask about the use of office spaces.

While working in an agency, the space you are assigned can vary. In
some agencies you might have your own office, while in others you
might share them.

When sharing offices, agencies sometimes provided individual cubi-
cles to store your supplies. In one location, we shared rooms, but we did
not have space allocated to us, so we often moved around. This was not
only difficult for clinicians but for clients. In those difficult situations,
good communication and relationships with peers was critical. I often felt
like a nomad with my supplies in my backpack. With this type of situation, having a laptop and cell phone enabled me to sometimes complete
my work remotely. Of course, *Health Insurance Portability and Accountability Act of 1996* (HIPPA) issues are important to address.

One of the benefits of working with an agency is that they put the
work into developing standards and security around the use of these
tools. I was able to benefit from this to make my work easier and still feel
confident I am following HIPPA. Password-protection availability of
your computer or cell phone are some of these concerns. Some agencies
lock down phones/computers to ensure the confidentiality of your clients. When looking at full time work with an agency there may be other
benefits that are offered that you would not have in private practice. For
example they may include medical, dental, vision, group life and AD&D,
long-term disability, voluntary life and AD&D, voluntary short-term disability, 401(K) plans, and/or an employee assistance program. Some
agencies also offer educational and training opportunities.

Working for both an agency and university can be a great mix. A
challenge I have found is that classes are generally scheduled for the
same time that are prime times for clients. Again, the balancing act comes
into play. Flexibility is required to be able to do both. The extra income
from teaching classes can supplement an agency salary. When you work

for an agency you gets paid less per client, and if you work in a nonprofit agency, it is even less. The upside though is you get paid regardless of if a client shows up.

When working with an agency, there may be limitations to what you can do outside of the agency. For example, there might be a no-compete agreement. In this case, you might not be allowed to see clients outside the agency. If you leave, there may be limitations to what you can do or be limited for a period of time to continue to practice. They might also require an agreement that you not teach outside the agency. When you interview, you may want to check if there are limitations.

There are varying scenarios that describe the predictability of teaching a class. When dealing with undergraduate level and general education requirements there is a larger group of students who will attend and a larger variety of classes to choose from. In this scenario the registration can be difficult and there is a greater likelihood that a class won't fill up and could be cancelled. If you are teaching at a career college where all the students go through the curriculum as a group or cohort, there is less likelihood of cancellations. If you are working on a graduate level, classes will be more predictable and scheduled in advance. Classes are more likely to be filled. Each institution pays differently, with some universities requiring a minimum number of students for you to receive full compensation. When there is low enrollment, they might cancel the class or pay a reduced amount, while some others have a flat rate they will pay for each class. Sometimes as student enrollment goes up the compensation goes up proportionately. One will want to know how payment for classes is distributed. Another thing to ask when looking at working for different universities is if they offer any benefits other than salary and liability insurance. Some may offer health insurance based on course-load.

There is a direct relationship between the above management of classes and the class syllabus. I learned to list the syllabus as quickly as possible. Students sign up for classes based on requirements and expectations of the professor. Unfortunately, one could put a lot of time into writing a syllabus and setting up the class only to find out at the last minute that it was cancelled. One does not get compensated for the time invested, so be careful not to count on compensation for a class in case it gets cancelled or does not fill up completely.

TRANSITIONING JOBS

The work of therapy requires flexibility, to meet diverse people, to work with diverse presenting problems, and to be prepared to adjust to the human temperament daily. When transitioning between the role of a professor and a clinician, similar skills apply. In both providing therapy as well as teaching, you will work with a variety of personalities and learning styles. How you make sense of the world and learn is going to be different from the way other people do. It is important to meet both clients and students where they are and help them learn and develop in ways that make sense to them.

As an educator, you teach and speak a technical language and might teach undergraduate and graduate students, requiring bringing information at different technical levels to a variety of people. As a therapist, you are trying to bring technical information to a level that is understandable to a variety of different people at developmentally different stages. A real joy of being a clinician and professor is being able to teach students in the language of the profession, but also be able to talk with them about how to translate that knowledge for their clients.

As a therapist, I was originally hired for an agency that had several locations. At one point, there was a consolidation of locations and a new administration emerged. My independence as a clinician, drive to work, and use of my own play- and sand tray-room changed. It was an uncomfortable adjustment that forced me to reevaluate my tasks in the agency.

Sandtray is a very specific type of play therapy. It can be more directive or non directive in nature. In order to do sandtray you need to have a container of sand and miniature toys. Some therapists use a basic storage box while others use a specialized sandtray that is on a base. The miniature toys fit into the container and depicting a variety of categories. For example, people, animals, buildings, vehicles, vegetation, fences, signs, natural items, fantasy, spiritual-mystical and so on. A large variety allows a client to express the metaphors that are most meaningful to them. Sandtray is a great way to help the client tap into their unconscious and experience the world in a new way.[3]

Fortunately, when working for this agency, in spite of the changes and challenges, I was provided an opportunity to apply for different positions and locations before they hired outside of the agency. This is an example of the on-going challenges agency work provided me, but I ended up enjoying the new responsibilities.

Another item to consider when transitioning to a new job or new agency is the agreement of length of time you have to give before leaving the job. Many times, two weeks' notice is standard; however, in one position, I had to give thirty days. This can be tricky when applying for new jobs. This is important information to explore when applying for a job.

REFERRALS

Referrals are different in a university setting as opposed to in an agency. Other professionals market and attract students as well focus on student retention, and the institution is responsible for setting class schedules that are often based on the needs of students.

Referrals for a therapist in an agency is a major issue. Without continued referrals, there is no job. In therapy the service you sell is yourself, your work, and your reputation. When you have been working for a period of time, referrals are generated based on your reputation, and old clients will refer to you. When you are a new clinician, it can be difficult and time consuming to get your first clients.

Working for an agency has several benefits. It is not just your reputation that you are selling, but that of agency's as well. In an agency, you do not have to worry about developing a name, which allows you to focus on doing your job. Building your name without worrying about the next referral is a tremendous relief. Agencies also understand that the services being offered are only as good as the therapists they hire. In this scenario your reputation could be connected to other therapists as well as to the agency. If they have a good reputation, you can count on residual benefits and increased referrals. Once you have been in an agency for a length of time, your work will speak for itself. In time, it becomes easier to make transitions within the agency or even private practice.

The types of referrals you receive will depend on the type of agency you work for. If the agency specializes in children, obviously referrals will be for children; if it is a general practice, you will get a variety of cases. Even in a general practice, there are therapists who will specialize. Your specialization is a critical item to consider when developing your skills in an agency.

When specializing you can become automatic, rigid, and inflexible when working with clients. While I specialize with children, adolescents, and their families, I discussed with my supervisor that I wanted to serve a variety of ages. In this way I stayed fresh and challenged. When I see mostly young children, I find it refreshing to add in some adolescents. When I have an opportunity to do this work with adolescents, I focus on talk therapy, get a different perspective, and work with more metaphors. At the same time, I do not see clients that are outside of my specialty; the shift is too significant and does not allow me to focus on my learning and mastery.

In agency work you will share referrals. In one agency I had people return whom I saw previously. Clients I see will also refer friends and family to me. The majority of referrals are available for all therapists in the agency. The supervisor assigns cases and tries to balance caseloads and refer to the most competent clinicians.

CASELOADS

There are a few things to keep in mind when discussing caseload in an agency. First, it is the agency that sets one's caseload. One's supervisor could be monitoring it as well as assisting you to have enough referrals to keep a minimum caseload. Agencies will sometimes set a quota that you will need to meet.

In one position I was expected to have 26 billable hours with clients every week. When the agency merged, the requirement dropped to 22 and has since gone up to 23. Even if you start a position with one expectation, as time goes and the finances of the agency are reviewed, that expectation may change. With the drop came more management of our work. We now worry more about meeting quotas.

The best way to meet agency expectations is to over book. For example, when I was required to do 22 billable hours per week, to reach that goal knowing that I have four to five cancellations or no shows per week on average, I booked more than the amount required. On some weeks there are more cancellations, and I get to catch up with my paperwork; on other weeks, they all show up, it makes for a challenging week. The goal is to find a balance. By knowing the population you serve, you can plan ahead. For example, the highest level of cancellations and no shows is in the Medicaid population. Another with similar rates is court-referred services related to custody issues. As a seasoned clinician, I have a greater variety in my caseload and the no shows and cancellations are fewer than the newer therapists. Newer clinicians will be doing more of the work with the high-conflict divorcing parents, which is a private pay and Medicaid business. Both types that are more likely to cancel or not show for their appointments. These therapists have the greatest challenges with finding a caseload that they like and not burn out. They also have difficulty keeping their billable hours up.

The issue of caseloads does not apply to a university outside of the number of students in one's class. The number of classes one teaches and the frequency depend on the university. While there might be a major difference between the frequency of classes and the number of students in each university, there are trends. It is important to understand these to plan classes or organize material. In an indirect fashion, this can also dictate if your classes will be popular or not, which would mean fewer cancellations.

PLAY ROOM

When working for a university, the play room is not an issue unless you are working for a program that offers play therapy. In that case, they may have a play room or rooms that are outfitted to train the students. For most institutions, you will be in charge of the play supplies needed for teaching. Setting up before class and cleaning up will be the responsibility of the professor.

At one university where I taught in the Master of Counseling program, it did not focus on play therapy, and so there were no play rooms or supplies. Nevertheless, it is critical to expose master's level students to play therapy. It is time consuming and labor intensive to set up play supplies, but there is no better way to introduce them to play therapy than to help them experience the toys and the process themselves.

Play rooms in an agency can vary greatly. Always check with the agency about their resources and whether they are willing to expand. Agencies that work with children and adolescents usually have resources for a playroom and supplies. The existing play room might not be set up the way you prefer, and replacing toys might be an issue if there is no budget for supplies.

One agency had rooms that served different functions. There was a play room, a sand tray room, family rooms, and individual rooms. Understanding the lay of the land always helps when planning for your clients' needs.

It has been great to have different rooms to use accordingly. I have appreciated having separate sand tray and play rooms, as it helps with the mess and clean up. There is also less stimulation. When I have had one room for both, it was difficult to keep the toys in categories. They were often used for sand tray *and* play purposes, especially when using non-directive play therapy.

Furthermore, a separate sand tray room helps open clients up. Often when I had one room, adolescents did not want to be seen in the room because they were not kids. However, they were more open to the sand tray toys when the concept was explained. It was difficult to bring adolescents and adults into the room as well because of size. Another consideration with the play room are the table and chairs. If sized for kids, which is small, adolescents and adults might feel uncomfortable.

It is also important to consider who will use the play room. If is reserved only for those who are trained in play therapy, they will see the space and toys as sacred for children's work. If they are used by anyone who works with children, the space and toys take on a different meaning, such as an art project. Having things put back in the wrong place or objects being taken from the room might also occur. In these situations, it could be stressful for a child. I have taken pictures of the playroom to help other therapists know where to put toys, so children are comfortable with the continuity. Educating other therapists about the sanctity of a play room and its toys is also helpful. A safe play room is also where children can depend on everything they need being where they found it the week before.

ADMINISTRATION

When working for a university, you are responsible for all administrative tasks related to the class, whether it is the initial administrative items or continued responsibilities while the class is in session. Grading, documenting, and keeping records of assignments, for example, are the professor's responsibility, but recruiting for or scheduling of classes is the university's.

Retention of students and at-risk students are major concerns for universities. One works in conjunction with other university personnel regarding this population. The university is responsible for the overall degree program. As an adjunct professor, you will have an employee of the university that you report to. This person could be the department head or an advisor to the program and is usually supportive. Regardless of your role customer service is expected and important just as it is in therapy or any other job. In this case the customer is the student. You will work integrally with the student and other personnel to make sure the student is satisfied.

In agencies, administrative responsibilities, such as handling phone calls, vary. In some agencies, a front desk takes calls and forwards them to you. When there is no front desk, you need to do this task on your own. You should give clients your business card with your direct phone number, as it helps them contact you directly. Scheduling is another area that can vary. In some agencies, clinicians schedule for themselves. However, in one of the agencies I worked for, a front desk person took my calls and helped me reschedule. I also scheduled my clients with a shared calendar. The more I utilized the help, the more it provided time to focus on the clients.

Paperwork is another area of administration. The agencies assign, and the clinicians complete the paperwork. Agencies audit files and track paperwork to see if work is getting completed, and outside organizations sometimes audit files to help with accreditation. This means that you submit regular audits of files and procedures to assure that the agency is meeting all regulations and requirements for the program. When I worked on my own, I did not have to do in-depth rating scales to assess progress, nor did I have to complete satisfaction surveys. In my current agency, though, I complete these forms because they are required for accreditation.

As problems arise, always return to the person whom you are responsible to. Sometimes, your direct supervisor can help with the problem, but reporting to upper management might be the protocol. Some agencies might not be responsive to your concerns, so it is important to flesh out these areas before taking the position.

INTAKES

The issue of intakes does not exist with universities, but personal referrals do in agencies. They can come through the front desk, and, once assigned and depending on the protocols of the agency, some clinicians can schedule their own clients. Always remember to return calls to potential clients within 48 hours. Many potential clients will call several therapists and schedule with the first person who contacts them.

Intake formats and implementation also vary. There are industry standards for intakes, specifically diagnostic assessment summaries and treatment plans, and there are also insurance standards. In addition to these, there are agency standards. These factors will dictate the length of the intake, but I try to complete the task in one-and-a-half hours and in one session.

Insurance companies dictate who must be in the intake session. If you are billing services for a child or adolescent, that client needs to be in the intake session. Even though I would prefer to interview the parents alone to discuss issues that are not relevant to the child, such as finances, disagreements, or court proceedings, I nevertheless need to follow the insurance company's protocol. However, I might afterwards meet for some time with the parents. Although we know it is clinically best to have the child in the entire session so there are no secrets, we have to adjust accordingly. If I need to meet with a parent separately to address sensitive information, I do two things. First, I assure the child that we will have time alone. Second, I assure the child that the information we are talking about has to do with the parent.

RELATIONSHIP BETWEEN CLINICIAN AND ADJUNCT PROFESSOR

Students sometimes complain that a professor is out of touch with the clinical world, but for me, being a clinician and professor complement each other. When I teach a class, I use real-world examples. The down side to this, however, is switching roles from counselor to educator and back. Being focused on play therapy for so long, I often struggled with adjusting my speech and vocabulary from counseling to the classroom, and vice versa.

The stay-at-home mom with young children will often state she needs to be around adults so she can remember what it means to carry on a conversation. Going from the playroom to the classroom I felt much the same way. I spent so much time putting things into child-friendly language that I forgot what the professional language was. When I started teaching, I felt a great excitement at being able to use professional language. At the same time, I was able to share with students how they can use this information in a practical way with their clients, giving real examples of adjusting the language.

How we talk in our master's programs and the concepts we utilize become a coded way of speaking to others. Outside the industry it might not be understood. I teach students in their internship how the professional jargon is confusing to many clients, and we talk about how to translate their professional language to match a client's level of understanding.

My work in a university helped me be refreshed and up to date on the research and literature only to enhance the work with my clients.

NOTES

1. Risë VanFleet, *Filial Therapy: Strengthening Parent-Child Relationships Through Play*, 2nd ed. (Sarasota, FL: Professional Resource Press, 2005).
2. See Erik H. Erikson, *The Life Cycle Completed: A Review* (New York: W. W. Norton, 1982).
3. Linda E. Homeyer and Daniel S. Sweeney, *Sandtray: A Practical Manual* (Clawson, MI: Self-Esteem Shop, 1998).

THREE

Variations of a Theme

Private Practice

Amy Hyken-Lande

I love when one reads a book and the main character decides to open a business. They hang up their shingle and boom, they are wildly success-ful! Got to love fiction! In real life, there is a back-story with a great deal of blood, sweat, and tears that is a part of setting up a successful practice. Hopefully, after reading my journey, you will learn ways to set up a *group* private practice, while being an independent contractor.

When one is in graduate school, they learn a plethora of important information. The focus is on theory, policy, practice, and interventions, and provides opportunities to test out different internships. Although the information that we learn, and the hands-on experience is invaluable, they do not teach us about the *business* side of the profession. Basically, they do not teach us how to get from point A to Z.

After four years of undergraduate school, three years of grad school, two internships, 3,000 hours of supervision and taking a very long test to earn my Licensed Specialist Clinical Social Worker (LSCSW) credentials, I assumed that I was ready to go. I started my therapy career as a clinician at a residential treatment center. I was part of a multi-disciplinary team and the head Social Worker for the adolescent unit. It was a great place to start and to learn. As a state-funded agency, there were a lot of challenges politically and clinically, so I was unable to focus on a specialty. I had to see all of the patients in my unit regardless of presenting problems and of my training. At the time, I had a few colleagues who were venturing into private practice. I hoped that one day I too would be able to start my own practice. However, I had no idea how to begin. It seemed like a huge leap. The idea of setting my own hours, not having to deal with the politics of an agency, and seeing clients that I wanted or in whose needs I specialized seemed like a goal that would only happen *one day*.

After years of working at the residential treatment center while networking with various mental health centers, I was offered an opportunity to join a group practice, which was another step closer to my goal. The group practice offered some of the freedom that I desired. However, I was still given clients even if I did not specialize in that area, and I had to reach someone else's quota. The money was better but not significant enough. In addition, 90% of my clients were in-home. I was spending an exorbitant amount of time and gas money driving around the city. I had more control over my career but not to the level that I wanted.

One day I was getting my nails done and was chatting with another customer. Her husband had a private practice and had an office to rent. I was excited about the opportunity of being part of a practice, but I was also scared to death. I met him and decided it was worth the gamble. I started with no clients and worked as an independent contractor but still had the feeling of being part of a group. He gave me administrative support and advice. I continued to work for the group practice to pay my bills, and having the income from that practice allowed me to make a plan and start transitioning to the new practice. My group practice was in a different state (Missouri), so I was starting from scratch in Kansas. Therefore, I had to find ways to get my name out there, so to speak. We negotiated the rent, and it increased as I became more established. I was succeeding by making lists of administrative and clinical challenges. One must have a blueprint to succeed. Several years later, we moved to a larger office and I took over the administrative responsibilities.

REFERRALS

The first order of business was creating referrals. This is something that you do not learn in school. I knew what type of caseload I wanted to develop: working with children who had trauma and anxiety. I wrote letters to social workers and school counselors. At the time, I was only on the Medicaid (insurance) panel; therefore, I focused on Title XIX schools. Title schools (*Social Security Act of 1965*) provide funding for medical and health-related services for families with limited incomes through Medicaid. When I received a referral from these schools, I immediately contacted them to collaborate on the case and let them know who I was. Following up with referrals always sustains and builds your practice. When I referred clients to other providers in cases in which I did not feel as qualified, it always helped to encourage reciprocal referrals. I also joined several networking groups which increased my referral base.

Speaking engagements were also a good way to market my practice and put myself out there. I also wrote a "Dear Amy" column for a magazine. These were not paid gigs, but they paid off! After several years, I expanded by specialty and began working with children of divorce. My advertising audience became the courts, attorneys, and guardians ad litem. In a year, I had established a financially stable practice as an independent contractor.

MOVING TO A NEW OFFICE

In moving to a new office, several changes occurred. I took over the administrative duties, which entailed finding an office, negotiating with the rental company, decorating, furnishing and remodeling, and informing clients of our move. I found other providers to be part of our practice; however, they still acted as independent contractors. If you are considering subletting to other clinicians, there are several things to consider. First and foremost, you need to share your vision to the potential roommates. The other providers were going to be part of our practice but separate; this means that they would share space, pay rent, be responsible for their internet and phone, as well as billing, and in turn would receive nonguaranteed referrals, monthly supervision, and be part of a larger successful practice.

As the saying goes, you live and learn. The first clinician/contractor that joined the practice did so without a formal contract, which was my first mistake. I naively assumed that we would discuss the guidelines and shake hands. In less than sixty days, we had given her clients and support, and then she moved across the hall. Lesson learned. We now have a brief contract. We make sure that while we are a group-like setting, support, supervision, and the possibility of client referrals have no guarantees. We want our contractors to be successful, so I spend time giving them ideas about how to set up a practice and market themselves as well as answer any questions they may have. At the end of the day, though, they are their own bosses.

As the administrator of the group, I had a challenging role. I needed to interview potential contractors, create an office contract, and define what it meant to be an independent contractor under the umbrella of a group. Fun things like doors not working, ceiling leaks, and temperature control also fell under my role. Schedules between contractors had to be spelled out, especially if you had more than one therapist sharing offices. I encouraged scheduling conflicts be worked out between therapists. However, if there were a stand-off, I made the final decision.

Even though contractors are their own entity, they are still representing the practice. In other words, you do not want just anyone subletting from you; you want to have reputable people as your roommates, not just someone who can pay the rent. In addition, as mentioned above, providing supervision assures that the contractors are seasoned and ethical. One also has to be willing to help them with completing their forms and navigating insurance, if needed.

CASELOADS

The topic of caseloads opens up numerous areas of discussion. It is a great segue into another foreign topic, and something that they do not teach in school. Insurance panels. To be or not to be, that is the question. For health providers, credentialing is the process of getting networked with insurance companies (panels).Some clinicians only take clients who have insurance, while others only take private pay. From my experience, one should have the best of both worlds. When I started my practice, I was only on the Medicaid panel. It took some time to become part of other insurance panels, so I began accepting private pay. While doing so, I had to decide on fees and how my sliding scale worked. Some insurance panels were open and easy to get on their panels as long as you were willing to complete the overabundance of paperwork. Other panels were closed, and I had to wait. However, while playing the waiting game, I could still participate, but only as an out-of-network provider.

While you are trying to decide on insurance challenges, you must consider billing issues. While this might be your least favorite of duties, you still need to get paid. There are several options: You can do it yourself, hire a billing person or company, or purchase billing software. Some billing software allows you to record progress notes and create schedules. If you are planning to work part-time with a small caseload, doing your own billing is the best choice. If you have a larger caseload, you should check out other options.

Your caseload is based on several factors and is unique for each provider. Besides your financial needs, you need to look at your emotional capability. Some providers can see seven clients per day, while others can only see four. If you spend the day seeing all trauma clients, you need time to process your emotions. To avoid professional and personal burnout, you need to manage the caseload. Remember that paperwork such as assessments, progress notes, and treatment plans, also consume time.

In some cases, you may share clients with another provider in the practice. For example, in a divorce case I may see the children, while one of the other contractors meets with the parents. Being under one roof makes it easier to coordinate services and consult; it also makes it easier for the clients, but requires coordination of time.

A DAY IN THE LIFE

It would be helpful to take one through *a day in the life* of a clinician in this setting. When a potential client contacts you, there are several things to consider. You must spend a few moments on the phone talking and listening to the client, or parent of the client, obtaining some basic data (for example, name, contact number, age, insurance, presenting problems) to determine if you are a good fit. This part is administrative and it allows you to accept or reject the referral or refer the client to another contractor in the office. Giving the other clinician the material you have collected is always helpful. Afterwards, I always ask the other contractor to confirm that they have set up an appointment.

Let us discuss the initial intake and assessment. There are many forms you can use for the intake session. Some insurance companies require specific information, such as demographics, medical conditions, past psychiatric treatment, and current functioning, so collecting a social history is essential. In this setting, each clinician has their own intake forms. At the first meeting, clinicians should explain their role and the limits of therapy. Following this, a discussion on the client's needs such as frequency of visits, completing *Health insurance Portability and Accountability Act of 1996* (HIPAA) forms, consent of treatment, fees and no-show policy will be addressed. The information gathered will help in formulating the treatment plan.

THE PLAY ROOM

Depending on your office set-up, therapists may have their own office or play room. In some cases, we have shared a playroom, while another option in this setting is creating a mobile play room, where you bring your own tool box. Something to consider is the design of the lobby or waiting area. It sets a tone but should not be a play room. It needs to be inviting but not therapeutic. You want the play room to be inviting, calming, and child-centered. It should be a place where children feel safe and are able to use their imagination, a place where they express themselves through toys.

One should be very deliberate when selecting toys, objects, and centers for the play room. Items to include: doll houses (ideally two houses, as many clients have two family homes), dolls, clothes, furniture, and plastic or wooden food. Being culturally sensitive is essential. For example, dolls should come in all shades. Puppets and felt story boards are also beneficial. Books and games to assist in expressing feelings in a non-directive manner, such as Legos, "cops and robbers" toys, and doctor items are necessary. Construction paper, markers, crayons, child scissors, glue, and other art supplies help children express their feelings. You want clients to feel safe and secure, so considering the use of sensory toys such as Play-Doh, slime, stuffed animals, or sand is important. You can use the sand tray for an initial assessment, as well as during the therapy process. It allows the client to show you their world. Cars and trucks, animals, people, and other miniatures should be used. You can also add rocks, jewels, trees, walls, fences, and other items that may relate to their home or school.

Hopefully by this point, you feel more secure and better informed. There are many things to consider and think about when you are making the leap to becoming an independent contractor. Even more, if you plan to share that office with other like-minded therapists. Write out your blueprint by using a vision board and to-do list, and take one step at a time. Now, go hang up your shingle!

FOUR

Navigating the Challenges of Being a Parent and a Play Therapist

Amy Badding

Being a mom of four has its challenges independent of being a play therapist. As my children have continued to grow, their idea of what their mom does for a career has changed too through each stage of their development.

When my children were young, they had no real grasp of what I did for a living; however, around the age of six or seven years old, an awareness emerged. My own children used to come to my office and play with the toys while I did paperwork, answered emails, or organized files. They loved to come with me and often begged to bring a toy home, which I allowed but let them know it needed to be returned the next day. While too young to understand, they did not ask questions; they just knew "the rule."

Once they started elementary school, usually around first grade, the questions began. When they saw other kids in the community—at school or at the grocery store—say, "Hi, Miss Amy!" they asked why. This is when the conversations about where I went every day while they were in school began. "Mommy, how do you know that girl (or boy)?" My blanket response was, "They are a friend of mine." My children probably thought, "I have little friends, and so does my mommy." No more questions asked, right? It was not actually that easy. Kids are very intuitive, and at the age of nine or ten years old—third grade—they started to put the pieces together, and the questions changed to, "Mommy, is that one of your clients?" How do you explain to one's children that you leave them every day to *play* with other children? Here's how:

1. Read to your child *A Child's First Book about Play Therapy*, by Marc A. Nemiroff PhD, and Jane Annunziata PsyD. This is one of the best books to help kids understand the job of a play therapist. It also helps them understand the importance of confidentiality. You can simply tell your child that your job is like the therapist in the book. Here is a very good way to explain what it is that you do: "I am a therapist to kids. I help kids and their parents when they have big problems that they can't solve on their own. They come to me for help. We talk, we play and talk, and we learn how to solve their problems. They trust me to help them and tell me things they may not tell anyone else. I have a very important job."[1]

2. Read books to your child about trauma and other childhood problems. These types of stories can help your child understand that kids have problems that they or their own parents cannot help them with and that they need me to help them navigate through this problem to have a happy life. Some of the books that I have read to my own kids to help them understand are: *A Terrible Thing Happened*, by Margaret M. Holmes; *Kids Need to Be Safe*, by Julie Nelson; *Blueloon*, by Julia Cook; and *Silly Billy* by Anthony Browne.[2]

3. Help them understand the importance of confidentiality just as you would explain confidentiality to your child clients. I let both my clients and my kids know that I take confidentiality and the stories they tell very seriously. What they say in the therapy room stays in the therapy room; in fact, I have a sign above my door that reads, "What you say in here, stays in here." Their problems and stories are only for me and them to know.

4. Have a conversation with your children telling them that Mommy cannot tell them how she knows these kids or their parents and caregivers. Most uncomfortable is when they come up to you at a store or sporting event, wanting to talk or even just to say hello. Kids understand that if I tell other people about them, they will not feel safe coming to my office. Try putting it into a situation that your own child may experience, such as, "It's kind of like when you talk to the teacher about a friend who is not being very nice. You don't want to get that friend in trouble, so you ask the teacher not to say anything and the teacher keeps her promise."

The play therapist who lives in a small community may have an even more difficult time with these issues. My community has a population of about 58,000, and I have many clients in my kids' school, whether learning in their classrooms, playing on their sports teams, or pursuing friendships.

CHALLENGES OF LEAVING ONE'S WORK AT WORK

When dealing with emotionally disturbed children who have experienced trauma, struggle with behavior issues, or are extremely anxious, it can be emotionally challenging. It is difficult to leave the office and not carry the burdens of others into your own home. In the car ride home, I process my day. I revisit difficult sessions and review an email or phone call from a caseworker or teacher, but I remind myself that I cannot do anything to fix the problems right now—I am done; I gave my all today. Although we talk with adult clients about displacement, this mental shift from work to home life can be challenging. Are we good at practicing what we preach? Not always, but it is important to use this time to breathe, listen to music, or talk to friends instead of continuing to work.

BENEFITS OF AND SUGGESTIONS FOR BEING A PARENT AND A PLAY THERAPIST

There are benefits to our career choice, I promise. The best part about having my own children and being a play therapist is that I get to take unwanted toys to work. This cuts down on the cost of buying toys for my play room, and I feel less guilt about the money spent on a toy that my children played with first.

Additionally, being a parent and a play therapist helps me relate to parents. When I began this career, I had two young kids and only minimal experience as a parent. Now, at the time of writing this chapter, I have a teenage daughter in high school, a boy in middle school, and two girls in elementary school. I can relate to a parent who says, "They play on their video games all day," or "I tell her to get into the shower five times before I hit my limit and have to yell." I have often thought that I know how this parent feels, but I have learned that it is not beneficial to relay personal experiences even if I believe I connect to them. I do not offer this information since the therapeutic focus should not be on me. I actually do *not* know how this parent feels; I am not in their shoes, and their experiences may be very different from mine. How their parents raised them, their financial considerations, or even the physical demands of their environment could have contributed to their own emotional responses. Additionally, they need my help, not my disclosing about my kids. Our circumstances are very different, so relating to them as clinicians and not as parents is more valuable.

Some of my clients know that I have my own children. Although I do not have pictures of them in my office, they nevertheless will ask about them. Some parents have said, "I bet your kids are the most emotionally stable kids in town," and I can easily answer with, "No, not even close." I am human, and I have made many mistakes with my children. However, I continue to learn from these mistakes.

Sometimes, we play therapists are much better in our offices than we are at home. We do not have the same responsibilities that we do at home, and we may be more present in our offices, more focused on what the issue is and what we need to do to help. I am often more motivated there, even if though it may be because it is the beginning of the day and I have already had my one (or two) cups of coffee. I occasionally feel like I am terrible at helping my own children at home. My husband will often tell me, "You're the therapist. Can't you fix this?" I then feel conflicted because I think I should be able to fix the problem, but I sometimes check out emotionally and avoid the issue. I struggle to parent just as the next person, but sometimes the expectation is so high by others that I just want to look the other way. Play therapists who are parents just have to do the best we can and not have unrealistic expectations of ourselves.

Despite trying to implement these suggestions, occasions arise that are taxing. My daughter once told me that I am "never home." She was upset with me telling her that she could not go to a sleepover. My heart broke when I saw the list of "sleepover activities" in her backpack that she would be missing. It is these moments that make me second guess what I am doing and how it affects my kids. Missed games and sporting events, seeing your child picked up last at daycare—the guilt. I have chosen not to give up my career goals, but I still sometimes envy the stay-at-home moms. I wish I could stay home and be happy, but I have accepted that my work is a very important component of who I am. Helping children as a trained play therapist is part of my destiny.

ANALYZING ONE'S OWN CHILD'S PLAY

I do not do this much anymore because I just do not have the time to sit and play with my younger girls. We color together or play cards before bed, but they often play together while I am doing the laundry or dishes and getting things ready for the next day. I was much more of a playful parent with my two older children. Then, I practiced my tracking with them and conducted a Marshak Interaction Method (MIM) on both while in my early training days of play therapy and Theraplay.[3] My son was a "sorter;" he would line up his Thomas the Train cars, play on the floor, and watch the wheels turn. He liked his toys organized and did not tolerate messes. My daughter did not play with baby dolls or Barbies. She was more active and preferred kicking a ball, riding her bike, or doing something creative and hands-on, such as crafts. It is funny to think about it today because this still describes them as teenagers.

As play therapists, it can be very easy for us to become alarmed by a child's play if it is overly aggressive or sexualized, and for good reason. If this happens in one's own child's play, then allowing one's child to play through these emotions just as one would a client can be difficult. If one has concerns about one's own child's play, emotions, or behaviors, it is important to seek external professional help. These are times when one cannot be a parent and a play therapist; these are times when one needs outside help. Connecting with another professional in one's community would be to one's advantage.

My son was once having trouble at school in second grade. I was getting emails about his behaviors and his inability to focus and listen in the classroom. I knew it was time to make the call for help. I needed guidance from another professional, and reaching out for help was a good decision for our family.

SELF-CARE

A mental-health therapist should find time for self-care, especially if one has children. A play therapist who works primarily with children and families can experience an increased amount of stress. One's counter-transference, when a therapist's feelings toward a client becomes more emotional or takes time away from their own family or other clients, can be challenged when extra time is dedicated to communication and collaboration with parents, school personnel, daycare providers, and others involved in the child's life. These issues may also be closely aligned with one's personal life.

My night stand is stacked with books about child therapy, but a novel sometimes appears in the pile to provide a much-needed break. Through the years I have developed neck pain. The mental and physical stress of sitting on the floor and leaning forward in my chair to connect with the child have challenged my body and soul. To that end, I realized I needed to review the books about mindfulness and relaxation techniques we teach to our clients. Practicing mindfulness and meditation have helped me relieve this pain, and so has diffusing essential oils in the office, which I have found helps the clients too. As a runner who has finished four half marathons, I understand that physical exercise has given me focus and relief from stress. Some ask how I find time, so I answer that I schedule, just like I teach my clients. I schedule workouts in the middle of my work day, and working in a group/private practice affords me the flexibility to do this. However, working in an agency might be more of a challenge. Balancing being a mom of four children who are active in soccer, basketball, baseball, and gymnastics, and trying to find *me time* is an on-going challenge.

RESPONDING TO DIFFICULT QUESTIONS

I have had children say they wish I were their mom, and this is difficult to hear, for many times these children do not have a positive mother or parent figure in their life. My response is, "So, you'd like it if I were your mom," reflecting their feelings and using them as a therapeutic opportunity to explore their perception of grownups. I explore what they are missing in their life, what they *need*, and help them to find solutions. I often help the parent or caregiver understand their child by saying, "It seems your child wants or needs more attention. How about a ten-minute date with them once a week?"

Children living in a troubled home often want to know more about me, my children, my husband, and my life. Trying to direct the attention to their positive qualities can be difficult because possibly no one has given them this much attention. I will often turn the attention back to them or incorporate a game that will help both the child get to know me and allow the child to talk about themselves. Many of the *get to know you* games are games that the child already knows how to play but with a slight twist. Such as matching the color of the CandyLand game to a question (such as, I like to . . .) or writing questions on Jenga blocks (such as, What is your favorite color?).

Children will sometimes ask me "is there something wrong with me?" or "why am I always bad?" Children with a history of trauma or behavior issues, are given attention by others when they are acting out or displaying negative behavior. Sometimes these kids don't know how to act "good." I have even had a child tell me, "It is just *too* hard to be good." This comment made me think about what they may feel on a daily basis. They are so used to making bad decisions that making good decisions and receiving positive praise are probably scary for them. I think of it this way. When you were a child and did something wrong in the classroom, what did you feel? It likely caught your attention, your face may have turned red, and your palms got sweaty. It was uncomfortable and you thought, "I will never do that again" because you did not like the way it felt. This is how the troubled child feels when they do something good and the response from the adult catches them off guard and causes them to freeze, they may think "I don't understand this feeling so I'm not doing that again." Troubled children need to learn what feeling good, happy, and excited is like and to practice it so they are not afraid to feel this emotion.

Working with children in the foster care system is heartbreaking. Children will often ask me if they will ever live with their mom and dad again. This is a question I cannot always answer, but I will empathize with the child by saying, "you are worried that you won't get to live with your mom and dad again. I don't know the answer to that question but as soon as I know, we can talk about what the judge decides and talk about it together." Children need to know the truth. So many people are trying to keep things from the child because they do not want them to be traumatized, but, keeping information from the child only creates more anxiety and stress. They need to be prepared and communicated to about what may happen, so they are better able to cope with it before, during, and after. I often tell parents to be honest. If they used drugs and need to go to treatment, it is ok to tell the child this but explain it at their level, which is something I can do to help both the child and parent.

IN CLOSING

Making the decision to pursue a career helping other people's children can be a rollercoaster of emotions both personally and professionally. It is not an easy decision to make, as one must make sacrifices between family and career. Working with young children who are hurting and who need a consistent professional in their lives to guide them can be difficult to manage when one has a family at home who needs them too. In the end, we can only give what we are capable of giving; less would not meet our *standards*, and more would wear us down. Finding a balance is the key to one's success.

NOTES

1. Marc A. Nemiroff and Jane Annunziata, *A Child's First Book about Play Therapy* (Washington, DC: American Psychological Association, 1990).

2. Margaret M. Holmes, *A Terrible Thing Happened* (Franklin, TN: Dalmation Press, 2000); Julie Nelson, *Kids Need to Be Safe: A Book for Children in Foster Care* (Minneapolis, MN: Free Spirit, 2006); Julie Cook, *Blueloon* (Chattanooga, TN: National Center for Youth Issues, 2012); and Anthony Browne, *Silly Billy* (Cambridge, MA: Candlewick Press, 2006).

3. "Tracking" is a child-centered play therapy skill where the therapist reflects and describes what the child is doing in their play, so the child feels that the therapist is fully present with them. The therapist does not "play" with the child, they are only interacting with them through their tracking responses. The Marshak Interaction Method (MIM) is an assessment tool used prior to using Theraplay as a treatment method with the child and parent. When conducting the MIM, the therapist observes the parent and child engaging in activities together from for dyads: Challenge, Engagement, Nurturance, and Structure. Sessions are then planned according to the dyad that may need the most work in the relationship between the child and parent.

FIVE

In-Home Therapy

Jacquelyn Thompson

I graduated with a master's degree in social work (MSW) in 2007, and my first job shortly thereafter was in an agency that did both in-home and clinic work. I am still working at the same agency and have experienced in-home therapy, from my own clinical experience and as a supervisor. When I first started here, it was a small building with very few offices, and so many of us had to do in-home therapy. After several years, I *earned* an office within the agency but still focused on in-home therapy. In 2011, I became a supervisor and maintained a smaller caseload that still included some in-home sessions. My experience has helped me provide support to a variety of clinicians, especially those who do in-home therapy.

In-Home Therapy is a modality where therapy is done in the home of the client. This modality is preferred by referral sources because the client is not making significant progress in traditional office therapy; the issues are due more to the home environment or because a barrier to therapy is transportation. In-home therapy is a unique modality that is not universally accepted and about which graduate schools do not often teach. Many students do not realize this modality is even an option until they are either placed in agencies for internships or begin working in settings that promote this modality. It is often their first exposure to in-home work although it can prepare them to move into other settings, such as private practice, because it teaches them to be more flexible with sessions and therapy and sets them apart from other clinicians. Additionally, it can build one's expertise and talent since it is so distinctive and effective.

LOCATION

An in-home clinician does not necessarily need a physical site to practice, as locations can vary depending on the client's home. The agency I work for has an actual building that is centrally located in our city. This headquarters lowers the cost of travel since it limits the amount of driving required to provide in-home therapy (for example, cost of gas, wear on the car). The agency has some offices available for clinicians to use when they do sessions in the office as well as provides a computer lab, receptionists, a billing department, an electronic-medical record system, office supplies, and even some helpful therapy games and resource books for its clinicians. This site also offers supervision for provisional therapists.

This in-home approach can vary with regard to the cost and remuneration. My agency contracts therapists on a commission basis, which means that payments by insurance companies or cash payments by clients will decide the reimbursement to the clinician. My state's Medicaid has a higher reimbursement rate for in-home therapy on some sessions as opposed to in-office therapy. The agency I work for pays a percentage of the reimbursement to the clinician depending on their licensure and supervision needs. The percentage the clinician receives is increased based on yearly reviews. This type of pay structure can vary one's income as there are several factors impacting it including how many clients are seen and the type of payment source but one could expect to earn between $32,000 and $60,000 plus per year depending on licensure, payment sources, and years of experience. Our agency offers reimbursement for mileage for in-home sessions due to changes in the tax codes in 2019 and this may change again in the future. The agency also offers other benefits such as cell phone reimbursement and gym membership reimbursement for full time employees. Tax codes are always changing so whether you are working in an agency or in private practice, consulting with a qualified accountant would be beneficial to see what things are able to be claimed as deductions for your taxes.

When working out of an agency, clinicians will likely use its mailing address for correspondence and billing; however, when they are in private practice, they may want to have a post-office box, particularly if they are solely providing in-home therapy and utilizing their home as their office. This is also important if they are in private practice so boundaries can be maintained, and if the clinician wishes that clients will not have access to their personal address.

When clinicians utilize their homes as their office, clinical records should only be stored at that location with the understanding that *Health Insurance Portability and Accountability Act of 1996* (HIPAA) requires that the records be secured under at least two locks. An example of this two-lock system is ensuring that the filing cabinet that stores the records has a lock and that the door to the room that houses the filing cabinet also has a lock. Records may also be stored on a HIPAA-compliant electronic-medical records system. There are many programs available to agencies and individual clinicians alike. The type of program chosen will depend on the individual needs and financial availability for the clinician or agency. The agency I work for uses *InSync Health Care Solutions*, which is both a practice management and electronic-health care record system in one and is web-based, making it accessible for our clinicians everywhere. I have seen other programs such as *Advanced MD, Simple Practice, TherapyNotes, TheraNest,* and *AccuCare*. Many clinicians in my area consult with others on what they use or use a practice consultant to determine the best fit for them.

CONFIDENTIALITY

It is important to note that providing in-home therapy can be very different than providing in-office therapy, especially with regard to confidentiality. When one practices solely in the office, there is a greater control of exposure to other people and reduced chances of overhearing, possibly through the use of music in the waiting room or sound machines within the office setting. However, when one provides in-home sessions, there can be other members of the family present during the session. Finding a confidential place in a home can be challenging at times. This issue must be discussed at intake so that the clinician, client, and family can define the boundaries of the work and so that everyone understands the nature of the therapy and the limits of confidentiality.

REFERRALS

Referrals for in-home therapy can be created in several ways. One source is through family court or Child Protective Services. Psychiatrists, hospitals, and in-office agencies will also provide referrals to my agency, specifically to do in-home therapy. When working for an agency, it is hoped that its directors will conduct the marketing to develop the referral base although marketing oneself is another important consideration. When developing a private practice, setting up a business Facebook page, listing oneself in *Psychology Today*, creating a website, and contacting potential referral sources are additional ways to build one's referral base. Networking with other agencies in the community can also be beneficial. By working in an agency, referrals can come more frequently, and the clinician does not typically have to focus on this aspect of the therapeutic process.

CASELOADS

Caseloads can vary from clinician to clinician, and because payment is based on the number of clients seen, one's revenue will also vary. Essentially, the more clients one sees during the week, the greater the income that clinician can expect. Full-time work in my agency is considered to be twenty sessions per week. Something for clinicians to keep in mind is the amount of additional paperwork (for example, documentation, court requirements, session planning) and/or case management that will be required in proportion to the number of clients they see and the severity of each case. In the agency I work for, additional requirements of administrative work include working with insurance companies to authorize services, conducting clinical reviews, creating treatment plans, and contacting the referral sources regularly. These administrative tasks would necessarily fall on the shoulders of private-practice clinicians unless they decide to contract these services out.

ADMINISTRATIVE AND CLINICAL REQUIREMENTS

In-home therapy has some similar administrative and clinical requirements to in-office therapy. Intake paperwork forms (for example, releases, consent-to-treat, rights and responsibilities) are expected with both modalities. Diagnostic interviews and biopsychosocial assessments for treatment planning are also essential in both areas. Sometimes one's assessment will depend on the payment source. For example, insurance companies and state-funded programs typically have different requirements that do one being paid by other means. In the agency I work for, they have one set of paperwork for all clients and choose to follow the most rigorous requirements, which in our state is Medicaid.

In-office sessions allow the clinician to create specific, distinct locations for toys and the therapy work. However, in-home sessions often require more flexibility, creativity, and spontaneity to create a play room. Bringing well-defined toys, understanding what might be already available in the home, and being responsive to the reality of the house when they enter will help contribute to the success of each session.

SAFETY

Another important issue for in-home therapy is safety, of the client and of the clinician. Understanding the community in which each in-home session is conducted is important since, with some, violence can be a part of the children's and family's everyday life. Something as simple as knowing where to park can make all the difference in the world. It is further critical to inform others in the agency where one is going so if something were to happen they are aware of the clinician's location. However, it may also prove difficult to do so while still maintaining confidentiality.

When situations become destructive or aggressive, managing these crises can be very challenging depending on if one is conducting in-home or in-office sessions. When at the clinic, the behaviors can be contained in the office, and the clinician can elicit help from others. When sessions are in the home, the environment may often be contributing to the disruption or precluding control of the problem. I recall one session when I was working with a family, and the mom and dad started arguing. It escalated to the point that they were eventually yelling, screaming, and posturing towards each other. This, of course, triggered the child, who began mimicking their behavior, despite our working on anger-management skills with the family. I was able to get the child to use the skills we were working on and go to their bedroom. Luckily, I was also able to calm the parents down without having to bring in law enforcement. Had this session been in office, I would have been able to bring in other staff to separate the parties and work with each of them individually. Another time, one of my supervisees' clients, who had a history of assaulting their guardian, blocked the exit to their home. Although the client was small enough for the clinician to move them, this was a physically dangerous situation and could have led to possible allegations. The supervisee called me, and I informed them to contact law enforcement to assist with the situation. Even though the supervisee was able to deescalate the client and to eventually get them to move, the client was taken to the hospital for a mental-health evaluation due to the aggressive actions and statements they made during the interaction. Subsequent to this session, the agency decided that all future sessions with this client would be conducted in the office for the safety of all parties involved.

All staff in the agency I work for are trained in safety protocol. This includes learning how to employ non-violent de-escalation techniques, how optimally to position oneself in the home so nothing blocks the exits if at all possible, and how to identify possible safety concerns in the home. If something occurs during an in-home session the procedure is that the clinician will get to safety, immediately call their immediate supervisor to discuss the options, and then document the occurrence and steps that were taken in a critical-incident report. Some of the immediate options include calling law enforcement to handle the situation, or take the client to be evaluated at the hospital, or having the guardians take the client to be evaluated at the hospital. After the incident is over and the report is received the clinician will typically staff the case with their supervisor or other clinicians and make a determination if a referral to another agency is needed, a behavioral contract is used to continue services or if the location of services is changed to in-office for increased safety.

When a client has experienced trauma, one needs to be especially diligent in client safety. If there are limited places to conduct therapy in the home, I try not to conduct the session in a bedroom due to their personal nature and the increased risk to both the clinician and client. Many clients have experienced traumatic events in their bedrooms, and it is important to have a safe place for therapy. Having a play session on the front porch of a house has been successful when there are limited options in the home, and eliciting help from guardians has also been helpful to protect the child from re-experiencing a traumatic event.

One also needs to consider health issues when it comes to safety. Cockroaches, ants, and bedbugs can appear in some in-home settings. If our agency is aware of, or becomes aware of, any insect infestation, until the family provides proof they have remedied the problem, all sessions are conducted in the office. This is still the protocol even if the vermin concern is due to neighbors who did not provide a clean environment. Since one can never be completely sure if bugs are present, prevention is key: I try not to sit on the floor or soft couches or even bring in any of my bags; I will also spray myself with a mixture of peppermint oil and water prior to entering the home and again when leaving. Some clinicians, when visiting a particularly high-risk area, will bring clothes to change into upon leaving and will spray their car with a pesticide. They then put the dirty clothes into a plastic bag and keep it closed until they get home, when they wash them immediately.

CONCLUSIONS

Despite the aforementioned concerns, for the most part, my experience with in-home therapy has been safe, beneficial, and very effective. Being able to experience the family in their own setting has been informational in understanding the dynamics that play a role in their mental health and is also helpful for my treatment planning. Sometimes a façade is presented during in-office therapy, which may only be revealed or unraveled in the home. My ability to vacillate between these two modalities has helped me be an even more effective clinician and supervisor. The experience of in-home therapy has allowed me to think outside the box with regard to interventions for clients, both my own and when supervising others. It has also allowed me to expand my thinking and to probe for what other factors may be playing a role in the client's mental and behavioral health. Having a total picture is extremely beneficial to the success of therapy.

In-home therapy is an incredible approach to working with families. Having this expertise can help clinicians develop special skills that can set them apart from others, either when moving from an agency to another setting or when beginning one's own practice. Over the years, I have noticed that in-home therapy is being used more and more, and I hope this chapter will help expand your horizons.

SIX

From Private Practice to an Agency to a Clinic

Trials and Tribulations

Amanda Gurock

When deciding to open up your own mental health agency it is not only important to ensure that you have referrals but you must make sure that you have taken into consideration rent, insurance, and overhead costs. This chapter will cover all of the hidden costs that it takes to run an effective agency that therapists do not only forget about, but do not budget for.

RENT, INSURANCE, AND OVERHEAD

When going out on your own and starting your own mental health agency, the rent, office space, insurance, and overhead fees are what you must think about when designing your own place. These are the back-end essentials that push the idea of creating one's own business. It can be expensive and scary, but by being aware of this, you will have a better bottom line and know what you need to be successful. Knowing your potential expenses and planning a budget will help you know at what pace you need to proceed when going out on your own or if you have enough referrals to cover your expenses.

The biggest discovery I had was that no matter how much you prepare, there will always be things that come up, and you will not be prepared for them. You will always need money in reserve because there will always be a problem. A prime example is when the WiFi goes down. How does one fix it? How does one keep records while the Internet is down? How does one access files? When this happens, you need to stop seeing clients and get the problem fixed. This can take a couple hours out of the day, which is, unfortunately, an additional expense. You need to have a working office staff who will keep systems running, which is an area that is commonly not taken into consideration. Everyone focuses on the clients, referrals. and keeping a full schedule, but without a functional office, you cannot succeed.

At my previous agency, the rent, insurance, and overhead fees were all negotiated by the Chief Financial Officer (CFO). He was responsible for the budget of the agency. While researching and recommending financial successes for the agency, he would investigate pricing, compare them, and ultimately decide which options were the best. He would then present this to the Chief Executive Officer (CEO) and lawyer. The CEO would then deliberate and have the final say on the options. When it came to the final signing of contracts and negations, the CFO, CEO, and agency lawyer would be involved to ensure the owner's best interests were being represented. For example, the lawyer would advocate that the agency have the right of first purchase in the event the owners of the building sold it. Retaining a lawyer is critical in the beginning to protect the owners from being personally responsible if the business fails. The CEO plays a passive and active role in the agency. They must be aware of what staff is doing at all times but not micro-manage them. A CEO should be aware of everything that the CFO is pursuing and the options available. In the end, the CEO, who is normally the owner, makes the decisions. This is something you need to be aware of and be comfortable performing.

TRANSITIONING

Transitioning from one setting to another is a difficult decision, ultimately one that the individual needs to make on one's own, as many factors go into this decision. You will want to ask if you have outgrown your current location. If the answer is yes, you will need to discuss important items with staff. Although this decision allows the CEO to grow the agency, moving is difficult since it is a risky journey, about which your clients will need to be informed. When selecting office space, be aware of public transportation. This phenomena contributes to referrals and can increase caseloads.

There are many people that can help with a transition. The first support comes from your family. They will be greatly impacted by the decision to move locations, jobs, responsibilities, and they might have to help you find space, banking, or even additional staff. The next level of support comes from seasoned therapists, colleagues, and friends. Do not be afraid to consult outside resources. If the relationships were positive, past employers can help with advice, direction, and support, so do not alienate past relationships and connections. Upon completion, thank these individuals for their input.

Be prepared for both pre- and post-transitions. The day of the move, everything can go crazy. You may never be fully prepared for a transition, but by being confident that your decision is the right one, the challenges and obstacles will become more manageable. You always question the decision in retrospect, so give yourself time to enjoy the new situation.

You will always want to be aware of finances. Ensure that you have sufficient funds saved for a transition or that a loan has been secured. Having cash for the first and last month's rent, utilities, WiFi, and any other day-to-day expenses. Billing and collections should be set up prior to the transition since the cash flow can be altered, cumbersome, or delayed. This will naturally affect your ability to pay bills immediately or even as time passes, which will directly and indirectly impact your family. Prepare them. Sometimes staying with a present employer until you set up the new location or job can help in the transition. Of course, this is always dependent on their permission to maintain different work locations.

Transitions and change are difficult. Remember, you can do it! In the end it will all be worth it. Having faith that you can do it is essential. Keep in mind that transitions do not always go smoothly, and there will always be challenges. It may take approximately three years after a transition to return to financial stability.

REFERRALS

Creating an approach to increase your referrals is critical for your business, and marketing your company is essential. This can be accomplished by providing potential clients with the following integral information: who you are, what services do you offer, and how can they find you.

Create a marketing list to send emails, flyers, or postcards. It is also helpful to have an open house once you are settled. People are always looking for new programs and services, so it is imperative to let them know that you exist. You should also develop a website, as well as a pamphlet, that includes descriptions of your services, staff information, email addresses, phone numbers, and your locations.

You will want to make sure people can call the office and get an appointment in a timely manner. Many referral sources want service now, and not later, so waiting lists are not recommended. Your staff should use good customer service skills when handling referral sources.

For example, it is helpful to keep notes on people with whom you have professional relationships. When I worked with a state worker, I wrote down her name and her daughter's name. The next time I spoke with her, I asked about her daughter. She has been a consistent referral source due to this simple act of concern. This behavior also demonstrates one's attention to detail.

Additionally, when a complaint comes in, you need to address it immediately. Every complaint is important, and you need to take the time to address it. Referral sources and people in the community appreciate your concern for these types of issues and see that you are accessible. Finally, to keep referral sources happy, you need to keep your word, see their clients, provide monthly updates, and make sure documentation is completed in a timely fashion.

Sustaining referrals is about building connections with the referral sources. When you are responsive to not only client's needs, but also to others involved in the case (for example, attorneys, state workers), referrals will continue to send you clients. The challenge is training staff how to maintain these connections. As issues arise, as long as the CEO is listening and addressing concerns, referral sources will be impressed and loyal.

Sharing referrals is not encouraged. The only time a referral should be shared though is if family therapy is required and an additional therapist is needed. For instance, court-ordered cases often require additional clinicians. If a child is referred, it is considered best practice to have one clinician work with the individual as well as with family therapy. It is also suggested to have one therapist treat an entire family of children, so that the therapist has a good understanding of the family dynamics and is better equipped to provide family therapy. This also addresses issues of manipulation and of triangulation. If a parent is being treated at the same agency, then they should have a different therapist. In these situations, the child's individual therapist should be included in the family sessions to support the child's voice. Each client requires their own charts, and information shared requires *Health Insurance Portability and Accountability Act of 1996* (HIPAA) compliance.

The management of referrals can be challenging. Keeping oneself and one's staff busy and meeting contracted weekly hours requires a good deal of balancing and education. When a staff member struggles to meet their target counselling hours, it could be helpful to share your own referrals.

Encouraging them to take additional clients at other times to offset this imbalance is another recommendation. Always remember that cancelation and no-show appointments play into these calculations. When staff is meeting contracted hours and referrals are continuing, the creation of a waiting list or sharing with other clinicians may be something to be discussed within the agency. This type of policy should be discussed so they understand how they and the team work together to keep the agency soluble. Remember that both extremes, too busy or not busy enough, can be liabilities for an agency.

Customer service calls can be used when numbers are low. The CEO and/or designated staff can reach out to referral sources, old clients, and current clients. Soliciting feedback can be constructive, so embrace the observations and utilize them to improve your agency. Referral sources appreciate your attention to these issues and how you care for the clients. When that referral source sends a patient, contact them and let them know how you have used their suggestions. For example, I learned that a clinician took two weeks to engage a family and set up an appointment, so I informed my staff that the next time this source referred a family or a child, an appointment was to be set up within seventy-two hours.

Your original goals and vision will dictate the direction in which your agency grows. If you choose to build an agency that specializes in trauma, then many of your referrals will be identified with trauma. If you want to be an eclectic agency, a different approach will be needed. It will be critical to remember not to change your mission to fit referrals. Diversify when you can by ensuring that your staff is trained in many modalities, by not relying on only one referral source, and by accepting various insurance plans. If you want to specialize, do so, but keep to that specialty. Many agencies struggle with being good in one area, but then try to be the biggest. There is something to be said about being the best but not the biggest.

Practice patience. Referrals are fickle and can change at different times of the year. You need to be prepared and do not panic. Follow your game plan, continually evaluating to see if you have reached your goals, and adjust accordingly. Be prepared and comfortable with saying no to staff, peers, and yourself. Some CEOs fear that if they say no, people will not refer to them. This is a myth. Refusing a referral will show that the quality of services that they are accustomed to may not be available at that time. Do not put yourself or your staff in a situation that you are growing too fast and cannot keep up. Feeling that you are merely putting out fires creates a bad work environment for yourself and for your staff.

CASELOAD

Deciding on a person's caseload can be based on the model of payment and/or structure that you have set up with staff. If it is a salary position, then you should ensure staff's remuneration is covered by the number of clients seen. For example, a schedule may allow for ten hours per week for documentation, five hours per week for lunch, and twenty-five hours per week for direct client contact. If you have other programs and staff are paid on an hourly basis, you should require the same direct contact and a predetermined wage should be established. With part time staff, a similar calculation should be determined. In an agency, the Director of Therapy is the one who decides who gets what cases. It is the Director of Therapy who is knowledgeable about staff caseloads, appointment cancellations and no shows, and a clinicians availability to see clients in a timely fashion. The Director of Therapy can also assign the client to the appropriate staff member. The Director of Therapy, when managing the staff, can diversify the cases assigned to not only challenge the staff's caseloads but also to help deter burnout. For example, foster care cases require an enormous amount of work in coordination. This can be very frustrating, time consuming, and exhausting.

As with referrals, there will be fluctuations in caseloads. Although when hired, there is an agreed upon number of working hours for staff, there are times that staff will not meet those goals. The fluctuation of cases needs to be taken into consideration for both the administration and the staff. Both need to be confident that referrals and caseload will eventually even out. Once a case is assigned, the therapist needs to continue working with it unless there is a complaint or the therapist is unable to meet the needs of the client. Confidence by both the administration and the supervisor helps staff succeed. It is helpful to encourage staff to also take care of themselves. As the business owner or CEO, you need to prepare for all financial and clinical situations. For example, if a staff member is struggling to maintain or to engage clients and it, in turn, causes their caseload to decrease, perhaps providing additional training in the areas that they need growth would be beneficial. These are considerations, both financially and clinically, that an owner needs to be aware of.

The Director of Therapy who knows the staff's specialty assigns cases. The first goal is to assign the appropriate clinician cases. This also ensures that there are enough clients for each clinician. These matches require a talented and insightful director. This person can also help a new staff member become adjusted to the demands of the agency. A slow beginning in the number of cases is always recommended to ensure the competency of a new clinician.

Sharing a case load is not encouraged because of overlap of responsibilities on a particular case. It is best to assign the case to one staff member. For example, one could have three people in an agency working with one family; the mother could be receiving services from one staff member, a child could be seen by another clinician, and the family could be seen by yet another. All clients are on a different staff person's case load, needing their own chart and requiring signed releases, which is not required by HIPAA but is the best practice. For cases that need to be shared, it is important to meet weekly and to coordinate services despite differences.

The clinical supervisor/Director of Therapy is the supervisor of the therapists. They should provide professional development for the staff and address staff's needs and encourage them to complete initial and yearly diagnostic interviews and mental-status exams. Meeting with staff weekly is ideal. At these meetings, reviewing progress notes, discussing the case, and monitoring case progress should be the agenda. Caseload is also a point of discussion, and identifying areas of improvement and growth is critical.

SUPERVISION

The clinical supervisor/Director of Therapy should also ensure that established policies and procedures for the agency are being followed. Addressing disciplinary actions are also in this individual's job description. Separating clinical and administrative times can be a challenge for this professional.

Not liking someone on your caseload occurs. It is rare for staff to like every client; sometimes the match just does not work. This comes out in supervision with the clinical supervisor or Director of Therapy. Like any other concern, the staff member's concerns need to be considered. In supervision, the discussion of countertransference needs to be explored. Sometimes supervision and proper training can help the staff person gain a different perspective and confidence. In turn, the case can be appropriately staffed by that clinician, and the dislike for the client(s) can be ameliorated. At other times, it may be appropriate to transfer the case. When that occurs, a staffing is set up, and the case is transferred. If there are ongoing struggles with a staff member and their caseload or relationships within the agency are strained, you need to consider if the clinician is appropriate for the agency. Releasing a professional is difficult, but you need to keep in mind that as the CEO, your responsibility is to create a professional, safe environment for staff and clients. Openness, trust, and communication are the overriding themes that guide you in creating, maintaining, and promoting a healthy agency. In turn, a strong cohesive team, a productive agency, and a resource for the community will be established. As the CEO, you will want to be accessible to staff, create a positive environment, and manage destructive forces within the agency, such as gossip or triangulation among different supervisory levels. The irony is that our job is to create a family within our agency that is no different than the family we create in our offices with our clients.

The best advice with regard to supervising and administrating caseloads is to be open and honest. Encourage communication and staff accessibility to supervisors. In turn, positive energy, increased creativity, and production will ensue.

Ensure that clinical supervision is kept separate from administrative supervision. Clinical supervision is for clinical development. It must be a safe place to explore countertransference. This information cannot be used against a clinician during their administrative supervision or in a punitive way. Staff needs to feel supported. This clinical supervision must always occur weekly, and administrative supervision can occur at a separate time and needs to focus on enforcing policies and procedures, and maintain structure within the organization.

There is a connection between administrative and clinical supervision, but roles and time dedicated to each are different, the ultimate goal for both is professional development. Administrate supervision focuses on the development of a hardworking, dedicated, time-oriented employee, and clinical supervision focuses on the development of a confident, skills-oriented culturally-competent clinician. If the staff has the same supervisor for both administrative and clinical supervision, it is incumbent on the supervisor to articulate which supervision is being provided. For example, staff should have clinical supervision weekly at a designated time and administrative supervision at a monthly designated time. The weekly clinical supervision should focus on cases, growth, intervention, skills and general clinical education. Monthly administrative supervision focuses on contracted hours, documentation, billing, file audits, client surveys, and performance as it relates to policies and procedures. Administrative supervision review negative actions and disciplinary actions. What occurs in clinical supervision should not be discussed in administrative supervision. Clinical successes or challenges should not be evaluated or addressed in administrative supervision. The ability to separate supervisory roles promotes greater professional development and open communication. My advice is to be as exact with administrative tasks as with clinical. This is just as important as referrals, seeing clients, and providing treatment. The administrative area has no financial gain and in fact costs an agency. A mental health facility only has one asset: the people who work for it. A major difference between one agency and another might be how one manages the facility and how one treats staff, and thereby, how staff treats clients. Staff need to be held accountable, both clinically and administratively. It is a demanding balancing act, but by being realistic, caring, empathic, and hardworking, this journey becomes manageable.

THE PLAY ROOM

Our agency has a play room that is used for individual and family therapy and for visitation by families. All staff utilize this room. Initially, the CEO set up the original play room, but subsequently, all staff members were invited to enhance the room. Several meetings occurred that involved staff's input of selection of toys, games, and furniture. In the end the CFO and CEO purchased the items. Once all items were purchased, staff helped decorate and set it up to be child and family friendly. The CEO and receptionist were responsible for maintaining supplies, cleaning, and replacing broken items. Staff's responsibility was to clean up the area after each session and to inform the CEO and receptionist of needed items. Staff were also encouraged to create their office as a play room. With this arrangement, staff needed to inform the administration what they needed in their office, but they could also bring their own supplies. Since security sometimes can be a concern, each office had its own key, and the CEO had access to all offices, but privacy was always respected.

There are a variety of toys, supplies, books, and games in the play room. The play room is intended to be a safe place and to have access to toys that help children express themselves. Toys included cars, trucks, dolls, puppets, super hero figures, doll houses, sand trays, figurines, doctor kits, dress-up clothes, and balls. There are many different variations of each toy so that any child or family may identify with the toy. For example, there are African-American dolls, gender non-conforming figures, half-human/half-horse, cat and dog figures, and girl and boy dress-up clothes.

Art supplies consisted of scissors, pipe cleaners, paper, crayons, glue, cotton balls, clay, play dough, markers, glitter, and wooden clothes pins. The art supplies encourage creativity and the expression of feelings.

Books are also plentiful in the room. Families read together and discuss a book. Reading allows depersonalization which in turn can encourage a child to express their feelings with regard to a related matter in their life. Book themes include one's own feelings, manners, biting, hitting, secrets, talking about bad things, being different, adoption day, and more. Our books are colorful and attract the attention of the children.

The playroom also has an assortment of games, and these can help in following the thinking patterns of children and their parents. They provide opportunities to see how children and parents communicate, talk, interact, praise, and fight. The game, Beat the Parents, allows children to work together to beat their parents. Checkers allows thinking patterns to be revealed, and Chutes and Ladders takes a long time, which encourages patience. When playing Memory, the therapist can see frustration from the client and has a chance to provide encouragement. Therapeutic games are also available. Typically, children and families choose games that they are familiar with.

The agency play room is shared, and a Google calendar coordinates its use. Sometimes there are conflicts, but staff are responsible for working through them. The advantage to creating one's own play room within one's office comes in handy during these moments. It is the responsibility of the staff to leave the room clean and supplied. With regard to the communal play room, expect the worse: items broken and the room not clean. Often conflicting appointments will occur but encouraging the staff with good follow through and holding them accountable will help. Remember, the principles one uses to run an agency successfully can be employed when running a play room.

ADMINISTRATIVE RESPONSIBILITIES

There are many administrative responsibilities within an agency. The CEO drives the vision of the agency and is responsible to manage and delegate responsibilities. In this role, the CEO is the most active member of the team. You need to be involved with everything but not run everything. Delegating responsibilities is critical for success, so the CEO must be responsible for defining administrative tasks. For example, since the receptionist is the face of your agency who has first contact with clients, referral sources, and staff, you need to choose someone who is responsible for taking messages, collecting faxes, starting files, maintaining office cleanliness, office supplies, and ensuring that staff have what they need and want. You will also want an effective accounts receivable person who checks staff documentation and the billing of sessions. Knowing if insurance policies are active and that clinicians have collected proper insurance information is part of this employee's responsibility. Following up on rejected claims, checking on payment remittance, and informing therapists are also included in job expectations. The CFO balances the books; handles payroll, taxes, and unemployment and liability insurance; organizes accounts payables and claims; and provides monthly financial reports to the CEO to make sure that budgets are appropriate and that finances are as budgeted. Human Resources concerns and ensuring the following of policies and procedures normally falls within their job description. Administrative supervisors deal with staff concerns, hiring, firing, disciplinary actions, quality assurance, review of client files, conducting client satisfaction surveys, and ensuring that staff is meeting with clients and providing their contracted work.

Hiring and promoting an administrative supervisor is no different than negotiating any other position within an agency. The CEO and CFO meet with an applicant and discuss the roles and responsibilities and compensation and responsibilities. With new hires, they also need to inform the staff.

Conflicts are inherent when you have a varied professional clinical and administrative staff. Open, honest communication helps navigate these conflicts. Administrative staff need to report to the CEO, who needs to maintain an open-door policy, excluding billers and the receptionist. Encouraging a chain of command and directing individuals to their supervisor is recommended. Time should always be set aside to address these concerns, and a conflict-resolution procedure or grievance process should be in place for all administrative staff to follow. Staff members should be encouraged to resolve conflicts directly, but if they feel that they have tried this with no resolution having been found, then the supervisor should be invited to help as a mediator. Once an agreement has been reached, hopefully the conflict will be resolved. If a conflict continues, the CEO and CFO or Human Resources need to be involved. A disciplinary-action meeting might be considered, so having open communication in an agency always helps in resolving many conflicts. Additionally, having a protocol to address issues will also facilitate resolution of conflicts. The role of the supervisor or CEO should not be to find fault but to alleviate the situation by acting as a neutral party. Keeping this perspective in mind helps staff handle the conflicts.

INTAKE

The intake protocol for clients in our agency is as follows: The referral is assigned to the therapist after insurance is verified. Then, the therapist calls the family and sets up the intake appointment, which is scheduled with the family, the therapist, and the clinical supervisor/Director of Therapy. The day of the intake the family is greeted by the therapist and clinical supervisor/Director of Therapy. The family is then led to the play room or the therapist's office—the decision of the therapist—and all the initial paperwork is filled out in the waiting room. This first session consists of introductions, the explanation of therapy and of roles and responsibilities, and an explanation of issues related to confidentiality. Typically, the family and client answer the questions. The comfort level of the client is always taken into consideration when assessing the collection of needed material. Observing the interactions during the intake is crucial in one's assessment of the family, and observations are recorded. At the conclusion of the intake session, the next appointment is scheduled. The clinical supervisor and therapist in a subsequent meeting discuss treatment and diagnosis.

The intake process is decided by the CEO, following insurance and clinical guidelines, which take into consideration diagnosis, articulation of treatment goals and objectives, and appropriate follow through. This ensures quality clinical and financial success. The intake requirements and protocol are taught to all staff, as uniformity is required in the agency. All staff sign an agreement to follow this policy and procedure. A successful CEO will ensure compliance of policy, procedure, and billing. Much of this is accomplished at the time of intake.

Intake protocol fluctuates between administrative and clinical tasks. The administrative staff (that is, clinical supervisor, Director of Therapy) assigns the case, and the therapist schedules the intake. When the client arrives, it is up to the receptionist and the rest of the administrative staff to collect the paperwork. Once these administrative tasks are completed, the therapist and clinical supervisor begin the formal clinical work. Flexibility is encouraged in clinical interventions and tasks but not in administrative ones.

The CEO needs to identify the most stringent insurance intake procedures and tailor one's intake procedure to meet those expectations and requirements. This often will be accepted by other insurance companies. Ensure that one establishes a policy and procedure that meet billing and insurance guidelines and requirements and then encourage staff to be unique and creative with their own clinical talents when collecting information at intake.

My best advice is the following: (1) You cannot do this all yourself, nor should you need to. Take your time and build a solid team. They will help with the research and find the best options for your agency. Do not rush and do your due diligence. For example, make sure the location, office space, rent, and overhead fees are not only manageable, but also practical. Find a good attorney that you trust. (2) Feel and act confident. You will get scared, but do not sweat the little things. Take your time and make good business decisions, and you will and can be successful.

SEVEN

School-Based Therapy

Dianna Sawyers

Schools are a microcosm of our society. Our students depict the best and the worst of our world. Furthermore, they include some of the most vulnerable and susceptible populations. They often highlight the most challenging struggles. Schools in the United States have responded to these needs through school-based programs, such as hot breakfast/lunch programs, nurses, athletics, special-education programs, speech therapy, and occupational therapy. There are now mainstream services provided by both our public and private schools. Recently, mental-health services have become a focus. With this increasing awareness, clinicians need to be better trained and informed, as well as more active in bringing positive changes to children therein. This chapter will examine the barriers, benefits, and challenges in providing school-based mental-health services as a play therapist.

As a school-based therapist, you will be presented with many different challenges and unique experiences. It is essential to bear in mind that while each school in a school district will take on a culture and a climate of its own, there are some universal elements worth mentioning. Each school has a slightly different hierarchy, method of interaction between therapist and staff, ability to provide both physical and financial support, willingness to incorporate suggested skills and strategies, means of identifying students in need of services, expectations of the clinician, and even varying degrees of welcoming the therapist and the services provided. However, the clinician is governed both by laws and by ethics that dictate your behavior as well as elements necessary to the functioning of such an undertaking. Many of these elements will be expounded in this chapter, including successfully entering the school setting, establishing

61

and maintaining referrals and caseload, developing a playroom, shoul-dering administrative responsibilities, and conducting client intakes and discharges.

As mentioned above, each school will be unique in its climate and culture, which will directly impact many of these elements. As a result, your role and responsibility in each of these elements will be addressed from two standpoints. First, we will take the position that you are either functioning as an outside entity (that is, self-employed, private practice, or employed by an agency) or as a direct employee of the school.

FINANCIAL COMPONENTS

The financial component for a school-based play therapist is one of the most challenging issues. In more traditional settings, such as agencies or private practice, fees for services rendered are paid through insurance, self-payment, or a combination of both. However, this is not an option for schools, as funding must come from alternative resources. A limited number of schools can allocate a portion of their budget for mental-health services, and grants have sometimes been used to offset their cost. Final-ly, school-based play therapists can be employed by an agency, private practice, or a sole proprietorship to attenuate these concerns.

School Budgets

Schools can allocate resources in their budgets for a clinician to pro-vide mental-health services. A full-time clinician can become an employ-ee with full benefits, but this option is expensive for schools and less likely to be available due to expenses like malpractice or health insu-rance. Some schools partner with an agency who might be able to pro-vide these additional financial benefits.

Grants

Grants provide the most flexibility in funding a school-based therapy program. As grants vary in the amount of money allocated, length of funding, and the designation of services, schools can be creative in their pursuit of these monies. Identifying the grant recipient is also an impor-tant consideration.

An individual practitioner or an agency who owns the grant can have more flexibility in the allocation of resources. As the executor of a grant, you have the freedom to request money for service reimbursement, sup-plies for administrative needs (for example, computers, software, phones), supplies for play therapy sessions (for example, toys, art sup-plies), or even for continuing education of therapists. It is possible to have a grant for a therapist's salary and a second grant for supplies, technological needs, and continuing education. Collecting and reporting data is a significant part of managing a grant, and your ability to report quantitative and qualitative data as requested can help in future successful grant writing.

Schools can independently secure a grant for in-house therapy services and then connect with a clinician outside the school to provide these services. In such a scenario, the school holds the major responsibility in making decisions on reimbursement for services rendered. Monies not included in the grant will be the responsibility of the clinician.

Understanding how therapeutic services are provided is crucial to grant implementation. Typically, grants come in a block allotment. Occasionally, they are awarded in a fee-per-service fashion with a maximum allotment identified. In the case of block allotment, you/your agency/the school will be awarded an amount of money to provide the services. Sometimes flexibility with regard to caseload changes needs to be considered. For example, a grant for $75,000 to hire a mental-health provider to provide services in a specific school district for a fiscal year with no limitations on the number of therapy sessions can be a reality. This type of grant is perfect for the clinician desiring to practice full time within a school setting. Grants that are fee-for-services allow the freedom to establish your own fee; the drawback, however, is that when the maximum allotment is reached, the grant is over. Using that same $75,000 grant allotment as a comparison, a clinician would only be able to provide twenty hours per week of therapy sessions for the standard thirty-six-week school year. This calculation excludes an increase in caseload and summer services. This type of grant is more suited for a clinician who wants to provide school-based services on a part-time basis.

TRANSITIONING INTO THE SCHOOL SETTING

Transitioning from an outpatient office to a school can be difficult but rewarding. Regardless of the funding or the position, you need to evaluate financial obligations, acquire supplies, and identify new needs because of your mobile status. Consider the following before beginning this process: How many days a week and how many hours a day will you be in the school? Will you conduct therapy outside of school services? What will you do during the summer? What additional supplies/materials do you need, and whose financial responsibility is it? How will you keep and maintain records? Which office equipment will be supplied, and which needs to be obtained at a personal expense? How will professional expenses (for example, insurance, licensing fees, supervision) be provided? The answers to these questions and more will vary depending on whether you are is an outside agent or a school employee.

Outside Entity

If you are coming from an outside practice or agency, funding is probably through a grant. It will be important to understand if the grant recipient is the school, you, the agency you represent, or a third party. Understanding the grant and its provisions and requirements helps answer many of the above questions. Coming from an agency, it will likely be the responsibility of the agency to provide equipment and materials. Play therapy items are not usually provided unless directly specified within the grant. On the one hand, these materials are likely to be at your own expense, but an advantage of this is that these supplies and toys become your personal property that can travel with you should you move to another position or agency. On the other hand, items purchased under grant funding remain with the grant recipient. Sometimes schools who partner with outside entities are willing to provide office-related expenses such as Internet access, copy-machine privileges, or phone services.

Deciding to be a part- or full-time clinician in a school will impact your transition. Fulfilling a part-time position within a school while maintaining a part-time position in the original agency can present additional challenges; for example, travel time between locations can be excessive. Conversely, an agency can provide a location for summer sessions for school children. Full-time school therapists face their own challenges, such as encountering isolation and being away from routine interaction with other therapists. Additionally, the school is also your client. Professional boundaries need to be maintained between yourself and school personnel in these cases. Teachers sometimes serve as pseudo-parents and should be coached on how to adjust their approach with certain students. Much like guardians, teachers will not always like suggested changes and interventions. However, as your interactions with teachers and staff grow, you are likely to be viewed as a colleague. It is critical to keep in mind that you are not a coworker with school personnel. Since teachers and therapists view children from different perspectives, you can be friendly but cautious in developing friendships, as this can lead to dual relationships. This separation between personal relationships helps maintain a balance to allow these differences to function simultaneously and complement each other.

As a school employee, many of these questions are answered for you. Your schedule and responsibilities are set and defined by the school. A record-keeping system is in place, and your office needs are provided, but you might still be responsible for maintaining liability insurance, paying for licensure, and continuing education. The most significant difference between being a school employee and an outside therapist is your relationship with the school professionals. Your will now be colleagues with teachers and other staff. Your responsibilities extend beyond being a therapist, as your will potentially be involved with before/after school duties or assisting in achievement testing, putting the individual in a position of authority over students. Enforcing school policy and behavior expectations will also be part of the job. Blending these two roles, school staff and therapist, will take a gentle touch.

TRANSITIONING WITH EASE

You can do several things to make the transition from a current setting to a school easier and more successful. First, contact another school-based therapist with experience in your particular school demographic and funding source. School climates are greatly affected by things such as geographic location, school and district population, economic status, and social setting (urban, suburban, rural, remote), and many different configurations of these elements exist. Each produces a different approach to education and mental health. A seasoned school-based therapist can provide invaluable information before you begin a new job. Second, be aware of the flow of a school year. Experiencing the standard school calendar is critical to understand the magnitude of your new position. Schools function on a semi-rotating calendar of operations (for example, parent-teacher conferences, seasonal programs, holiday breaks, state-sponsored testing, other events unique to each school), which impact students and teachers, your access to clients, and the number of referrals. Finally, no matter how prepared you are, there will always be something that surprises you! This is normal. Learning to be flexible and resilient will help you be a stable and consistent force for clients, families, and school personnel.

Identifying students in need of therapeutic services is a critical task in successfully establishing school-based, mental-health services. Whether employed by an outside agency or by the school, educating the community and school staff about mental health and psychotherapy is essential. It is also necessary to recognize stigmas and biases around mental health issues, as well as general ideologies and cultural norms. Schools are governed by federal, state, and local laws, and this governance impacts the manner in which they approach and address both academic and non-academic challenges, such as mental-health concerns.

REFERRALS

Many of your referrals will come from school staff. For this reason, it is important to remember several things. First, many schools are governed by laws requiring them to become financially responsible for any professional recommendations made for nonacademic services. For example, if a school recommends a child be seen by a doctor, dentist, optometrist, or therapist, the school is financially responsible for transportation as well as all connected service fees. For this reason, many school professionals are hesitant to identify services not already established within the district. It will take time and education to help teachers and staff to accept and encourage additional services. Second, it is essential to develop positive professional relationships with the staff. They will be your source for referrals and are also in a position to measure progress. Finally, if you are coming from an outside agency or entity, remember you are a guest in the school setting; demonstrate respect, cooperation, and support for the staff.

Internal Referrals

Your primary source of internal referrals will come from the classroom teachers and school counselors, who are likely to initiate a referral based on classroom behaviors or due to a student's making frequent visits to their office. Be aware that as your professional relationship develops with teachers and staff, they will become more aware of what is and is not a concern needing therapeutic evaluation or intervention. Other mental-health needs beyond behavioral misconduct issues will also be introduced in this referral process.

External Referrals

Outside referrals come from many sources but account for a significantly smaller portion of referrals. Nevertheless, these communicate your talent, expertise, success, and availability to the greater community. Outside referrals can provide an opportunity to educate school personnel on the broader scope of mental-health concerns. Their view of you as a competent professional beyond the school system can have a great impact on their ability to listen to and then to follow your advice. Communication with parents and other community members can also generate referrals. Medical professionals, juvenile officers, and even students will support your work and speak of successful encounters. This helps increase your credibility in a community and in turn increase outside referrals.

A point of consideration: with certain funding, you may be limited in the number of outside referrals that can be accepted. Some grants have a stipulation that only identified concerns or diagnoses affecting school performance can be served. When documenting outside referrals and presenting problems, be aware of these requirements to renew or obtain additional grant funding. For example, if parents requests their child be seen due to a divorce, the school may see no problems. There may be no changes in behavior, academic performance may be stable, and peer relationships may appear intact; this would not warrant a school referral. However, the parents experience sleep difficulties, aggravated sibling relationships, and defiance at home. It is important to advocate for this client to receive services no different than a child who has become disruptive in the classroom and struggles with peer relationships due to a new baby at home but who is doing well in the home environment. This type of referral and documentation provides a clinician with an opportunity to educate school and funding sources about the need to provide services in spite of the limited definition of services.

Managing Referrals

Once you have a new client, it is your responsibility to review the referral and to contact the guardian. This is important for two reasons. First, you need to verify with the guardian that services are desired and that the guardian has given permission for such services. As most of your clients will be under the age of eighteen years, you will need consent to treat, a *Health Insurance Portability and Accountability Act of 1996* (HIPAA) release for the school, and any other paperwork required by the school and/or your agency. It is not uncommon for older children or teenagers to complete this paperwork without the knowledge of their guardian. In this case, be careful of forged documents, which might not be any different than agency or private practice requirements. Second, this contact will establish rapport with guardians. While the school setting provides comfort for many guardians, there are still stigmas around therapy and mental health. This will be a good opportunity for you to discuss the work you will be doing and to invite them to be part of it.

After making initial contact, you need to decide if it is an appropriate referral. Your availability as the therapist, the needs of the client, your training and expertise, the presenting problem, and the amount of additional resources, whether internal or external to the school system, need to be taken into account. If you work in a school where there is more than one therapist, you need to identify how referrals are to be divided. I have found that your interest and the availability of therapists to be the best criteria to divide labor.

My supervisor once asked if I wanted to be the best child therapist, or if I wanted to be the best therapist working with children experiencing a specific set of symptoms. As a school-based therapist, you will have to explore your personal answer to this question. While I feel most comfortable and confident when working with children who have experienced trauma, I know that I also have been trained and mentored with regard to children struggling with grief, making social connections, depression, or anger control. This is a critical professional growth question, and within the school setting, I have found it is easy to navigate this challenge. This will be a guiding force in determining which cases you accept and which you refer out. While some of your early referrals are likely to be behavior management, having struggled with this question will help you develop a wider base of skills. For example, on the one hand, a colleague was exceptionally skilled in working with individuals struggling with eating disorders, and she received these referrals. I, on the other hand, took a broader range of referrals, which allowed me to build a larger caseload.

A final aspect of referral management is when numbers are strained, which is either not enough or too many. Let us consider insufficient referrals. As a school therapist, you must remember that schools have a unique rhythm, which is different from outpatient services. Referrals hit a peak around October but then slow down. The next peak is about six weeks after the winter break. Many factors contribute to these two peaks, and you can do a few things at the beginning of the school year to increase your referrals, such as attending back-to-school night and being prepared to provide paperwork and give general information about your services. It is also important to contact the guardians of any student returning from the previous school year, as some grants only cover services during the school year. Even when given the opportunity to continue services through the summer, very few families take advantage of it. In my experience, fewer than 15% of cases will do so.

The opposite end of the spectrum is when referrals increase and you have no time. This, actually, is a good thing! First, it means you have established a successful practice. Second, it shows an increasing acceptance of using mental-health services. In these situations, though, you sometimes have to refer to others. Always be aware of other mental-health services in your area and how to refer to them. At this time, review your own caseload. In school settings, there may be long-term cases but fewer short-term cases. Know and understand which category clients fall into before accepting them. It is possible that a short-term case can turn into a long-term case. To manage a large caseload, try to have an idea at the beginning how long you expect to provide services for a client and what challenges might arise that demand additional time. Remember that clients often regress prior to the termination of services since it can be more difficult for clients in schools, as separation is not as precise as when conducted in an agency. Children see you in the halls and hear your name mentioned by teachers, staff, and other students. This can make it more difficult. Understanding this flow of referrals can be useful for grant reporting. If you are not grant funded, this data is helpful when discussing issues with the administration to increase, change, or decrease services for the school.

CASELOAD

Many of the factors that account for who is placed on your caseload and how it is managed will depend on the structure of the school. These differences are sometimes due to funding sources. Also to be considered is the professional title under which you perform your tasks. There is a difference between a play therapist, a crisis-intervention specialist, and a guidance counselor. Caseload is also connected to consent and HIPAA requirements. For example, in play therapy, the rules of consent change during a mental-health crisis. As a guidance counselor, you do not need guardian consent to interact with a student, but you likely would for prolonged intervention. These are items you need to consider in a school setting.

Ultimately, you are the professional and need to be in control of your caseload. Nevertheless, the size and fluctuation thereof, who supervises it, and whether or not referrals and cases are shared with other professionals, may not be under your control. If you are employed by an agency, you will likely have a supervisor or director setting these expectations. Grant-funded positions will mostly be concerned with all of these numbers. As a guidance counselor, you are less likely to have these types of controls.

Size and Fluctuation

As many school districts now include pre-kindergarten through twelfth grade, developmental stages will impact the number of clients to whom you can provide daily services, as well as the duration of services. Schools have expectations as to how long a student can be absent from a classroom. Furthermore, the amount of times a student is allowed to be absent from a class also needs to be considered. Given the standard parameters of a seven-hour school day, you could easily have six to fourteen sessions per day, with each session ranging between thirty and sixty minutes. The flexibility of each school and its administration will be a determining factor when establishing the number of clients seen daily and the duration of each session.

If you are funded through a grant, you need to develop a grant-compliant method of tracking the services provided and caseload. Tracking the total number of students served, the total number of service provision in hours and minutes, the total number of services rendered, as well as the total number of contacts in person or via telephone with school personnel or other service providers or team members are all means of doing this. Recording these numbers and tracking, both year to year and semester to semester, will also help illustrate fluctuation in your caseload.

Supervision of Caseload

Supervision of your caseload can be dependent on your license. If you do not have a clinical license allowing you to practice psychotherapy independent of supervision, you will need a clinical or administrative supervisor. A clinical supervisor can provide case consultation and legal guidance when needed. School counselors working towards a clinical license in school-based programs funded by grants can have the opportunity to fulfill their clinical hours to full licensure. Within these programs, discussion of supervision needs to be initiated. As an employee of an outside agency, your clinical supervision can be found within the agency. As a school employee, you might need to find clinical supervision outside of the district.

Administrative supervision, regardless of being a direct school employee or an agency clinician, will occur within the school system. This can be provided by a principal, guidance counselor, or special-education director, but it varies between schools.

THE "PLAY ROOM"

Since your location and accessibility as a school-based play therapist may vary throughout the day, flexibility is a necessity.

Creating a Play Room

Unless you are hired by the school with a permanent space designated for therapy, the play room will be mobile. When traveling between schools, you will always need to assess the supplies needed. Your theoretical approach should be the guiding force behind these choices, but you should also be prepared to make accommodations and adjustments.

The essence of any play room, mobile or permanent, is that it is a safe space. In the school, this brings an additional level of difficulty. Unwelcoming physical spaces, changing locations, and reminders of the classroom, such as desks and textbooks, can be barriers in creating this safe space. For example, sometimes you will have a unique setting, such as a supply closet or abandoned classroom. Consider using a rug, a large tablecloth, or a fabric shower curtain to define your safe space. All of these are easily washable, transportable, and are a size that provides enough space for you and your client. A small table with two chairs can provide an area to engage in art play or directive activities. Arranging the toy selection and/or art supplies in a similar fashion as in previous sessions can create predictability and stability for your client.

A limited toy selection is needed to accommodate a mobile play room. Always consider including nurturing, real-life, creative-expression, and relationship-building toys. Below is a list of suggested toys to include. When selecting toys, think about items that can play multiple roles. This helps in the transport and clean up. You must also consider the storage and display of toys. Small plastic storage containers the size of a shoe box are options for sorting and storing toys by category. This aids in display, as you can remove the lids and organize the containers in the same manner every session around the rug. This is also very useful when there are no shelves or permanent storage areas. Additionally, clear plastic allows the child to see contents from any direction.

Maintaining a Play Room

Maintaining consistency in your play space will be difficult. You will likely share space and experience frequent moves. It is, however, appropriate to communicate therapeutic needs and advocate for stability and consistency in the therapeutic setting for your clients. Communicating with your school about storing your toys and materials in a secure place is important, as well as communicating your needs to peers and the administration is critical in these settings. If you are assigned to a school for consecutive days, it can reduce preparation time. A large rolling duffle bag or very large reusable grocery bags serve well for transporting toys and materials. You may need to think creatively to use larger toy items such as a doll house. A game board wrapped with a large sheet of thick paper with four to seven squares traced on the paper can serve as a *doll house*. Remember, children need space to create each room. No artistic skills are needed here.

Another important element in maintaining your play space is understanding when, how, and with whom you will be sharing the space. It is our responsibility to protect the privacy of your clients and their play room. This may require the education of school staff and administrators that space cannot be shared while a session is in progress. To insure this, you may need to change locations throughout the day. Clients learn from our behaviors how we adjust to changes, too. If advance notice is possible, share with your client what changes are taking place. Being reassuring is critical. For example, you can say, "Good morning, Joey. I am glad to see you. Before we start walking, I want you to know we are going to use a different room today, but all the toys will be the same. Mr. Brady needed to have a special meeting, so we are going to help him out by letting him use our room." A simple exchange is useful when any change is made such as time, day, or when switching from directive to non-directive play.

Toy List

Real-life play and nurturing toys:

Doll house (or adequate replacement)
Doll-house figurines (multigenerational are preferred)
Stuffed animal
Baby doll
Bottle

Plastic play food
Plastic play dishes (two each: cup, plate, spoon, and fork)
Community helpers
Cars (at least four)

Aggressive Toys:

Ball (slightly deflated volleyball is ideal)
Toy Soldiers
Stress balls

Creative/Expressive Toys:

Plain paper
Construction paper
School Glue
Safety Scissors
Tape
Crayons
Markers
Water paint
Clay
Fidget toys/manipulatives

Relationship Building Toys:

Board Games (age and developmentally appropriate, preferred
    selection: Candy Land, Chutes and Ladders, Mancala, Checkers)
Card games (Uno and standard deck of cards)
Smaller foam ball

ADMINISTRATIVE RESPONSIBILITIES

In the school, it can be difficult separating between administrative and clinical responsibilities. Administrative responsibilities occur outside the formal therapy session. In schools, there are fewer administrative tasks than in agencies. For example, the recording of expenses and task of billing do not normally occur, whether funded by grants or being salaried although grant writing and data collection are required. Proper documentation, assessments, and management of client records are the administrative items you need to consider. However, administrative tasks vary based on how you are employed.

Documentation of sessions can be the most challenging of all these tasks. Completing paperwork during the school day can detract from the total number of clients you see, but completing paperwork outside of school hours extends your day. Additionally, to remain after school when you are not a school employee can also be problematic for the school.

Grant writing and data collection is essential in renewing grants. This success is dependent on the clinicians providing the required data. Grants have mid-year to annual evaluations. Qualitative and quantitative data is required for these reports. This data collection is an ongoing process and becomes cumbersome and difficult if you wait until the end of the school year to amass this data.

If you are employed by an outside agency, many of the administrative responsibilities are decided by the agency. For example, it will determine when session notes are completed, what is to be included in session notes, what types of assessments are used, how often assessments are conducted, what information needs to be gathered at intake, and which forms are used. As a school employee, you may experience similar requests but with less intensity and with more of your input. If you are self-employed, you will make your own decisions about these matters. Unless you are a school employee, documentation is not part of the client's school record.

Intake

Depending on your funding, the intake process will vary. Grants may require demographic information. The execution of the intake will not compare to a standard outpatient procedure.

For an intake in a school, you obtain consent to treat and the necessary HIPAA releases, gather a case history, and define the presenting problem. The most efficient means of obtaining this information is to send paperwork home with the child for their guardians to complete and return. Keeping paperwork to a minimum is also helpful. In the school, you might encounter guardians who are illiterate, do not have writing skills, or may not be native English speakers. These situations require the child to be a language broker for the guardian. If this occurs, finding someone to aid in this process is helpful for all involved.

It is critical that you contact the guardian prior to the first session with a child. This provides an opportunity to validate paperwork received, explain limits of confidentiality, establish rapport, answer questions, and describe the therapeutic process. This contact can be either be face-to-face or by telephone. This affords you an opportunity to gather information about the child without the child's being present.

At this time, it is important to assess if the child is aware that she or he has a scheduled appointment for therapy. In a school, it is not uncommon for a guardian to initiate the therapeutic process without the knowledge of the child. This could create an uncomfortable situation that could impact the relationship. Many young children become fearful if they are pulled out of a class. They believe they have done something wrong, so you will need to explain why they have been chosen, what will happen during your time together, and how to have them help you gather pertinent information. School or agency requirements will determine how much information needs to be gathered from the guardians and children.

Confidentiality is another important concept. Seeing a child in the school requires HIPAA releases from the guardian(s). Unless directed by the client or guardian to share specific information, you are expected to adhere to ethical principles and professional discretion to guide both the form in which information is shared and how much information is released. While it is natural for teachers to become concerned and even curious when their student leaves the classroom for a therapy appointment, the therapist cannot disclose the content of sessions. It is your responsibility to safeguard the privacy of your client and act in their best interest.

CONCLUSION

It takes time to adjust to the subtle, and sometimes not-so-subtle, nuances of being a play therapist in a school. A school setting will give you an exceptional opportunity to grow as a professional. You will learn new perspectives on the therapeutic process and will be privileged to work with an amazing population, one you may not have otherwise been able to serve. With all the changes and challenges, this is rewarding work. Being directly involved with schools gives you access to information not easily accessed. You have a direct connection to the school and home, and changes can be made in both environments simultaneously. You also have the opportunity to interact with and to influence adults in this social network. Children spend more time in the classroom with peers and teachers than they do with siblings and guardians, and so the success rate in this environment can be encouraging. Dispelling mental-health stigmas can be achieved in this work, and the impact you have on educators can be inspiring. You can play a vital role in creating generations of healthier youth.

EIGHT

Private Practice and Consulting

Allan M. Gonsher

My career as founder, head clinician, and director of Kids Incorporated for the past four decades laid the groundwork for my becoming a consultant. After more than twenty years of running my own clinic and specializing as a play therapist for children eleven years old and younger, I began to explore consulting, as I wanted to pursue an even more rewarding journey. I had the experience, knowledge of, and talent for clinical issues, and the business acumen to go on this adventure. My success story follows.

Consulting can look like an expensive, complicated, and overwhelming endeavor, but following in my footsteps by making sure to plan beforehand will help manage this anxiety. I believe practicing, teaching, and following the research in the field for a number of years before venturing into a *consulting* career is helpful. Let's be honest. Why would someone consult with someone who has had limited experience and expertise?

Financial issues were my first fear. I was concerned that transitioning from private practice to consulting would be cost prohibitive. I had originally thought that time spent away from the office meant lost financial opportunity, but I quickly learned that the prior success from Kids Incorporated's clinical work covered many of the expenses of consulting work. Why pay hundreds of extra dollars when I was already paying administrators at home? My secretary could answer inquiries and produce materials for presentations and could also manage my calendar while I was away. However, being absent from work for a day or two to consult required constant planning ahead. Tasks such as arranging transportation and lodging were assumed by this clerical team, and additional administrative tasks (for example, securing names, addresses, and telephone numbers) were delineated to other staff members, making weekly check-ins necessary to ensure responsibilities were completed in a timely manner. I needed my home base to run smoothly, and I also needed to assure current clients of my availability in case of an emergency.

Since I did not want to and could not afford to deplete the financial resources that I had worked so hard to create, ensuring cash flow continued was also a top priority. Balancing my clinical work and time for consultation could have been an obstacle, but I continued to maintain my caseload in spite of travel, still seeing between thirty-five and forty-five clients a week. Managing the monetary intake for my private practice helped ensure the viability of the burgeoning consulting business until it began to establish its own financial independence. Managing the financials of the practice required maintaining a consistent case load and ensuring that my colleagues maintained their caseloads as well. Sometimes creating additional referrals for the other clinicians, by directing them to doctors, school counselors, or old clients, helped maintain an even cash flow.

I was also nervous, as I am sure everyone is, about not finding clients who actually wanted consulting. There were many different venues I needed to explore to find these, which started out as a complicated endeavor. I first chose the Play Therapy Network and then began contacting state and chapter Association for Play Therapy (APT) (www.arpt.org). Although calling chapter presidents and board members was beneficial, it was a very competitive and time-consuming task.

I also chose to market myself as a speaker, so I began conveying my expertise in pertinent topics, such as trauma, gun control, and sexual molestation, which proved rather successful. It was a slow process, but after several years, I became a regular participant speaking at conferences. Initially, I was not the keynote speaker, who is almost always remunerated generously, but I eventually became well known. I can remember that starting out, I was responsible for all the expenses sustained in attending conferences. But after being on the circuit for some time, I could command enough money to pay for the fees incurred by attendance as well as cover the time absent from clients and the extra administrative expenses.

As stated above, colleagues were another source of referrals. Over the past twenty-something years, I had established many connections with clinicians and educators, so I decided to base the bulk of my consulting on referrals. By expanding my network of professionals, as well as increasing speaking engagements and doing more consultations, I grew my list even more. I would read articles, watch webinars, and go to seminars. I would contact the authors, presenters, and speakers and keep in contact with them, especially those who were doing similar work. This all contributed to my building a fluid referral network.

Once I had begun receiving consultations, I realized that the issues for which people sought me varied greatly. Many were business related and asked how to establish and maintain a private practice or how to secure a referral network. Topics also focused on management, such as how one should supervise or hire for an agency. Consultation issues were also related to clinical work, such as how to use a sandbox or to set up a play room. Some consultations were actually instructional in nature and directed or coached colleagues. I was often asked how to help others become consultants and engage other clients in consultation, and clients would ask me how to teach their peers to give webinars or how to provide a colleague supervision.

Since I was on the road, there was no such thing as a playroom when doing consulting. Everyone speaks about the playroom in their private practice, agency, or school, so I needed to create a mobile playroom, which included my favorite toys, including puppets, clay, and figurines. By using this mobile playroom, I could demonstrate play therapy wherever I was. After securing the appropriate releases and addressing issues of privacy, doing live seminars with children and families was easy and more authentic since I could create a playroom on the stage in front of an audience. This further helped in demonstrating a particular technique, procedure, or intervention. At one point, Kids Inc. had created a "traveling play therapy seminar" that covered seven states. This venture required hiring a marketing and public relations person, but it was an expensive ordeal and did not end up being financially profitable. The upside of this endeavor, however, was that it created even more contacts and exposure, which provided future consultations, clients, and supervision.

Some caveats to consider: Unless one aggressively publishes books, has a particular speaking niche at a particular time, or demonstrates expertise that is *buzzworthy*, one may quickly disappear into oblivion, with new and upcoming consultants, experts, and clinicians rapidly taking one's place. One must conduct thorough research. A good consultant, clinician, or speaker has about a two-year success rate and then will need to expand into other professional organizations. I would recommend that one check who the keynote speakers are and their topics at many of the professional conferences, put the data together over three years of that organization, and then see what names repeatedly come up. Whether you do it yourself or hire an administrator or marketing person, it is an expense though certainly worth it.

What has ultimately led to my success, was understanding that developing referrals for consulting work and finding speaking engagements is no different than developing my private practice: I need to hustle to connect with people. Relationships, relationships, relationships! One establishes one's name by networking and proving one's worth. Creating relationships is the foundation of this work. This could come as a result of pursuing social media, and it is certainly one of many vehicles one should use to expand one's contacts, but a more reliable medium is connecting with established names and organizations in the industry.

Although it has been a laborious task, it has ultimately paid off. In sum, consultations is a worthy adventure for imparting knowledge, not to mention that it helps one feel good about one's work and feeds into one's ego. Additionally, it can be lucrative, making it spiritually and financially rewarding.

Bibliography

Browne, Anthony. *Silly Billy*. Cambridge, MA: Candlewick Press, 2006.

Cook, Julie. *Blueloon*. Chattanooga, TN: National Center for Youth Issues, 2012.

Erikson, Erik H. *The Life Cycle Completed: A Review*. New York: W. W. Norton, 1982.

Holmes, Margaret M. *A Terrible Thing Happened*. Franklin, TN: Dalmation Press, 2000

Homeyer, Linda E., and Daniel S. Sweeney. *Sandtray: A Practical Manual*. Clawson, MI: Self-Esteem Shop, 1998.

Nelson, Julie. *Kids Need to Be Safe: A Book for Children in Foster Care*. Minneapolis, MN: Free Spirit, 2006.

Nemiroff, Marc A., and Jane Annunziata. *A Child's First Book about Play Therapy*. Washington, DC: American Psychological Association, 1990.

United States. Congress. *Health Insurance Portability and Accountability Act of 1996* (HIPAA). Public Law 104–191. 104th cong., 2nd sess. (August 21, 1996). 100 Stat. 248.

VanFleet, Risë. *Filial Therapy: Strengthening Parent-Child Relationships Through Play*. 2nd ed. Sarasota, FL: Professional Resource Press, 2005.

Index

AccuCare, 42

administration, 24; agency, 24, 28, 56, 58; consulting, 75; in-home therapy, 44; meetings, 5; private practice, 5, 29; school-based therapy, 72–74; supervision, 70; university, 24

Advanced MD, 42

agency: accounts receivable, 58; accreditation, 24; administration, 24, 28, 56, 58; appointment cancellations, 22, 53; assessing progress, 24, 30; benefits of working with, 18, 21; billing, 58; budget planning, 49; caseloads, 22, 30, 53–55; chain of command, establishing, 58; Chief Executive Officer (CEO), 50, 53, 54, 55, 56, 58, 59, 60; Chief Financial Officer (CFO), 50, 56, 58; child therapy, 21; clinical supervision, 54, 55, 56; complaints, 52; confidentiality, 18; contracting therapists through, 42; contracts, 50; customer service calls, 53; Director of Therapy, 54, 55, 59; educational and training opportunities, 18; emergency funds, 51; expectations of, 22; feedback soliciting, 53; general practice, 21; gossip within, 55; grievance process, 58; human resources, 58; in-depth rating scales, 24; independent contractors within, 5; insurance, 49–50, 58; intake, 25, 59–60; internships, 41; locations, 20, 60; marketing, 51; medical benefits, 18; meetings, administrative supervision, 5; meetings, clinical, 14; office space sharing, 18; outside work, limitations to, 19; overhead costs, 49–50, 60; payment models,

53; payroll, 58; play room, 10, 56–57; password protection of phones and computers, 18; progress notes, 30; receptionist, 24, 56, 58; referrals, 5, 21, 25, 51–53, 58; rent, 49–50, 60; reputation, 21; responsibilities, delegating, 58; salary, 18; scheduling, 24; sharing clients, 30; starting your own, 49–60; startup capital, 49; supervisors, 22, 24, 55–56; taxes, 58; transitioning to new, 50–51; treatment plans, 30; triangulation within, 55; vs. working for a university, 18–19; waiting lists, 51; waiting rooms, 7; website, developing, 51

American Psychoanalytic Association (APsaA), 8

Annunziata, Jane, 34

appointments, 11; cancellations, 22, 53; intake, 10, 31, 59; overbooking, 22; private practice, 7

Association for Play Therapy (APT), 76

Beat the Parents, 57

behavior issues, 35, 67

billing: agency, 58; insurance, 30; software, 30; system, 5, 6, 7, 29, 30; web-based, 7

Blueloon (Cook), 34

boundaries, 38, 64, 65, 66

Browne Anthony, 34

cancellation policy, 11, 22

career: Generation vs. Stagnation stage, 16; Stages of Development, 16

caseloads: agency, 22, 30, 53–55; assigning, 54; countertransference/ dislike of client, 55; fluctuations in, 54; in-home therapy, 44; private

intervention, 68; directories, 7; diversity in, 13–26; family, 18, 22, 52; filial, 14; general practice, 21; guidance counselors, 69; in-home, 13–14, 41–46; language of, 20; parenting and, 33–39; play, 14, 22–23, 69; school-based, 67–74; specializing, 6, 28; stigmas around, 67, 74

TherapyNotes, 42

transitioning/changing careers, 27–28; applying for new jobs, 20; giving notice, 20; group to private practice, 7; group to school-based therapy, 63–65; group to solo practice, 7; teaching to agency work, 19–20

trauma: children and, 35; client safety and, 46; responding to difficult questions about, 38; teaching children about, 34

websites, 7, 43, 51

About the Contributors

Amy Badding, LMHC, RPT, holds a bachelor's degree in Child and Family Services, Iowa State University, and a master's degree from University of Nebraska-Omaha (UNO) in Community Counseling (1997, 2007 respectively). Badding has worked for twenty-two years as a therapist in a variety of settings and positions, including her own private practice in which she specializes in working with children, twelve years old and younger, with mental health issues. She is the mother of four children and has worked as Certified Child Life Specialist (CCLS) for the University of Nebraska Medical Center; and also, with counseling agencies, group practices, elementary schools, and as an in-home therapist. Badding has also completed the Play Therapy Certificate Program at the KC Play Therapy Institute. Badding specializes in Child-Centered Play Therapy (C-CPT), Parent Child Interaction Therapy (PCIT), and Eye Movement Desenzitation Respond (EMDR). She also teaches online webinars for Kids, Inc. and provides live trainings on Play Therapy around the state of Iowa.

Allan M. Gonsher, LIMHP, LCSW, RPT-S, holds a master's degree in Social Work from Columbia University, New York, and is the founder and CEO of Kids Incorporated for more than forty years. He is also an internationally recognized speaker and guest lecturer who conducts workshops on play therapy techniques and provides consulting services. In addition to being the editor of this book, Gonsher authored *An Allowance Is Not a Bribe* (J. Aronson, 2000). He is a registered Play Therapy Supervisor and member of the Academy of Certified Social Workers, Association of Play Therapy, and Clinical Member of the American Association for Marriage and Family Therapy. Gonsher has been an adjunct professor at Mid-America Nazarene University in Olathe, Kansas, and guest lecturer at the Hebrew University School of Social Work in Israel. Additionally, he taught at the University of Nebraska School of Social Work, Drake University, and Creighton University. Play Therapist of the Year (1996), Social Worker of the Year in Nebraska (2001), and the Lifetime Achievement Award in Nebraska (2017), are among the many awards he received during his career. At present he is working with the Israel Association of Play Therapy. His passion during his career has been to provide direct services to children who are eleven years old and younger and to their families, as well as training generations of new counselors and social workers. He is truly a therapist's therapist.

Amanda Gurock, LCSW, graduated from Columbia University with a master's degree in Social Work. She lives in Albany, New York and currently works as a Pediatric Clinical Social Worker, where she helps children and families meet their personal goals and aligns them with needed services. After graduation, Gurock and her family moved to Nebraska where she worked with families and children involved in the foster care system and where she specialized in trauma. She specializes in Trauma-Focused Cognitive Behavioral Therapy (TF-CBT) and Child-Parent Psychotherapy (CPP) and uses these modalities to help her clients and families be successful. Prior to moving back to the East Coast, she ran her own successful mental health agency for many years. And, in order to keep things balanced in life, Gurock is also a certified spin instructor and teaches spin classes as she believes in a holistic approach in keeping one's mind and body healthy.

Amy Hyken-Lande, LSCSW, LCSW, has a bachelor's degree in Psychology and a master's degree in Clinical Social Work from the University of Kansas, and is a Child and Family Therapist. She has been in practice for over twenty years. She specializes in counseling children (for play therapy), as young as three years old through adolescents. Her areas of expertise include: children of divorce, reintegration, trauma/PTSD related issues (including physical, sexual and emotional abuse), domestic violence, anxiety, ADHD, social and self-esteem issues, and creative parenting skill training.

Julie Plunkett, LPC, LCPC, earned her master's degree in Counseling from MidAmerica Nazarene University in December of 2001 and went on to become a Licensed Professional Counselor in Missouri and a Licensed Clinical Professional Counselor in Kansas. She completed a postgraduate program in Play Therapy in 2012 from MidAmerica Nazarene University. She has gone on to focus on children, adolescents, and families, particularly those in crisis. She specializes in working with trauma, specifically with foster and adopted children as well as children of divorced parents. Additionally, she has received certification in Adoption Competency. She has worked with all ages of children and adolescents as well as their families. Most recently she was part of a program that worked with issues related to divorce and reintegration of a parent and their children. Plunkett has also served as an adjunct professor in both undergraduate Psychology courses as well as graduate level Counseling classes with her main focus being on internship, trauma, and family systems. She also has worked for years supervising students through their play therapy program and state licensure. She has a strong passion for children, youth, families, and education.

Yeshim Oz, LIMHP, is in private practice in Omaha, Nebraska. After teaching children with Autistic Spectrum Disorders in her hometown Istanbul, Turkey and elementary school children in Vienna, Austria for many years, she and her family immigrated to the United States. She received her masters degree in Counseling at the University of Nebraska-Omaha and worked in a public school as a school counselor for five years. Knowing her passion for psychotherapy, she joined a group practice before opening her own private practice in 2013. She attended many workshops on Play and Sandplay therapies and earned a certification from International Psychotherapy Institute for successfully completing a two-year training on British Objet Relations theory and practice. She is currently working on her certification as a psychoanalyst at the Greater Kansas City Psychoanalytic Institute.

Dianna Sawyers, MSW, LCSW graduated from the University of Missouri-Columbia with a Masters in Clinical Social Work with an emphasis on child welfare. She completed the Certificate of Play Therapy program at Mid-American Nazarene University. Dianna has practiced for 10 years, specializing in the use of Play Therapy within the school setting.

Jacquelyn Thompson, LIMHP, LMHP, CMSW, LADC, has been employed with the same agency in Omaha, Nebraska since 2007. She completed her bachelor's degree in Psychology at the Northwest Missouri State University in 2003 and her master's in Social Work at the University of Nebraska-Omaha in 2007. She currently is the Director of Substance Use Services, supervisor of interns and new therapists, and maintains her own caseload at the agency for which she works. Thompson has practiced for more than a decade as an agency therapist and is now a supervisor. She specializes in In-Home therapy, substance use evaluations, and dual diagnosis counseling.

www.ingramcontent.com/pod-product-compliance
Lightning Source LLC
Chambersburg PA
CBHW030656270326
41929CB00007B/389